THE SH  R

Small Green Circles

by Jean Aron

Revised
THIRD EDITION

**Dedicated to all my outdoor friends in Pennsylvania,
who share my enthusiasm for our home among the trees.**

* *

INVITATION

Whether you are new to walking in the woods, or a seasoned
long-distance hiker, this book has something for you. It is
particularly special for those who are short of time, short of breath,
or just short-legged. Whatever your length, just remember to
Keep Hiking, my friends, and keep it short!

FOREWORD

In 1982 when the first edition of *The Short Hiker* was published, there was a perceived need for this sort of information. Wednesday hikes were the highlight of the week for many of us. Our weekends were often spiced with longer hikes. The woods and trails were our constant delight, as we explored ever-widening "green circles" of our natural world, and formed "green circles" of friendship among hikers of every size and shape. But one thing was clear, both then and now: most people want more "SHORT HIKES". Families with children need easy, interesting places to walk. Students, teachers, and busy workers of all ages need to fit some fun into their schedules. Older folks need to stay fit with gentle exercise. Continuing demand prompted the publication of a Second Edition in 1994. In 1999 a steadily growing and changing community with a continuing need for hiking guides now prompts publication of a Third Edition of *The Short Hiker*.

* * * * * * * * * * * * * * * * * *

THE SHORT HIKER, Small Green Circles, 3rd ed. (C)1999 by Jean Aron supplements and replaces information written and published by Jean Aron in the first two editions:

- First Edition: 1982, titled, *THE SHORT HIKER, A Unicorn Hunter's Guide to Gentle Trails in Central Penn's Woods*
- Update to the First Edition: 1987, titled, *THE SHORT HIKER UPDATE*
- Second Edition: 1994, titled: *THE SHORT HIKER, Short Hikes and Gentle Walks in the Heart of Pennsylvania*

COPYRIGHT 1999 JEAN ARON, All rights reserved.
Published 1999 by Aron Publications,
227 Kimport Ave., Boalsburg, PA 16827

ISBN 0-9670597-1-2

ACKNOWLEDGEMENTS

- I wish to give thanks to my Wednesday Hiking friends from the University Women's Club, who have inspired and been the test group for these hikes;
- To the Centre Region Senior Hiking Group, who continue to explore new places for all of us to enjoy;
- To the Ridge and Valley Outings Club folks, who have given form to our dreams, and will continue to provide leadership to carry the standard of outdoor fun into the future.
- A word of special thanks to the volunteers -- from Keystone Trails Association and other hiking clubs and individuals -- who build and maintain hiking trails. You are the heroes, for without your efforts many of these trails would disappear.
- I am grateful to those who have taught me about the trees, the birds, the flowers, and changed the way I see and feel about this green circle of life we call Penn's Woods.
- Thanks to Mike Hermann of Purple Lizard Publishing for his friendly help and advice on making and printing maps.
- Most of all, I thank my husband, Gert Aron, who has provided me with 40 years of loving help and support, and has applied a steady engineer's hand to drawing the maps for the book.

* *

- Cover photo by Lois Chavern:
  "Hikers Enjoying Redbud Blossoms"
  at Canoe Creek State Park, May 1998
    - Back Cover photo by Ann Hettmansperger
      "Green Reflections on Standing Stone Creek"
      at Alan Seeger Park, September 1997

* *

DISCLAIMER: Neither the author, nor any group or individual mentioned in this book, is responsible for trail conditions, or occurrences on the trails.
Many volunteers do limited maintenance on some trails.
Every effort is made to furnish accurate, current information.
Drinking water sources are not tested regularly and cannot be guaranteed safe.
The hiker is solely responsible for his or her own safety on the trail.

MEET THE AUTHOR

Jean Aron has led a hiking interest group for University Women's Club of Penn State, University Park campus, since 1971. She knows a little about hiking and a lot about "short". A small person, 4 feet 9 inches tall, she is a personification of "the short hiker".

Jean is also a founder of Ridge and Valley Outings Club and is active with Keystone Trails Association, Mid State Trail Association, and Centre Region Senior Hiking Group. She is a member of ClearWater Conservancy, Western Pennsylvania Conservancy and Shaver's Creek Environmental Center. Her hobbies include birding and botanizing, x-c skiing, nature photography, playing keyboard, and writing poetry and music.

A native of Iowa, she and her husband have been Pennsylvanians since 1969. Their two grown sons live in large cities now, but enjoy returning to "small green circles" whenever possible.

PREFACE to the Third Edition

These hikes are arranged in the order of their location. All descriptions begin in State College, Pennsylvania. Why? Because it is located in Centre County, very near the center of the state, with good access to outdoor places. Besides, it is a place many of us call home, or at least headquarters.

A new feature of this edition will be the "Circle Number". Each area will be grouped according to the crow-fly distance from State College -- i.e. *Circle 5* means it is within a 5-mile radius; *Circle 10, Circle 20, Circle 30, Circle 40* means within 10-, 20-, 30- or 40-mile radius, etc. An index map shows the overall plan, with concentric rings (*Small Green Circles*) marking the distances.

Our goal is to make the book useful and concise (*short*), but at the same time it should provide everything a hiker needs to know about "where, what, and how" to find and walk these trails. The book should be entertaining and motivational as well. This is a "How To" book, but it is also a "Why To". We want folks to be moved to see, learn, enjoy and ultimately to love and protect these special places. The woods themselves will be our inspiration.

LOCATION KEY INDEX MAP

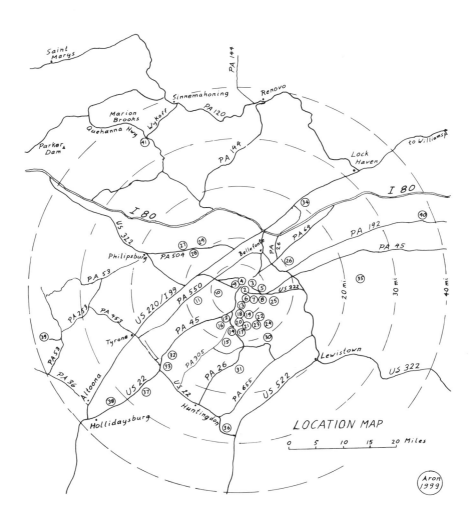

LOCATION MAP

0 5 10 15 20 Miles

Aron 1999

TABLE OF CONTENTS

      ****

CIRCLE 20

      ****

CIRCLE 30

      ****

CIRCLE 40

      ****

APPENDIX

A word on the organization of chapters:

      The Center of the circles is in State College, at the intersection of College Avenue (PA 26 N & S) and Atherton Street (US 322 Business E & W). All travel descriptions begin from that hub, and start on one of the 4 roads. Circle numbers indicate air miles or radius from the Center. The chapters are further arranged in each Circle by grouping together hikes which lie in the same general starting direction, i.e. PA 26 South or PA 26 North, or US 322 West or US 322 East.

            Circle 5 = within a 5-mile radius
            Circle 10 = within a 10-mile radius
            Circle 20 = within a 20-mile radius
            Circle 30 = within a 30-mile radius
            Circle 40 = within a 40-mile radius

INTRODUCTION

What is a short hike? A HIKE can be any sort of walking which is done for fun, especially in the woods. Some people like to walk fast and vigorously, and cover long distances. To them, any true and serious hike must be 10 miles or more. This type of hiking, where exercise is the chief purpose, can be a very enjoyable way to relieve pent up energies and frustrations. Your body becomes fit, and your mind becomes clearer, as problems shrink into perspective.

On the opposite end of the spectrum, a NATURE WALK is much slower paced. It may cover less than 1 mile, but be full of interesting things to observe. In fact, you will probably see more of nature by sitting still and letting it move around you. This provides very little exercise, but can be relaxing, delightful, and totally refreshing to the spirit.

The third possibility is a compromise between the vigorous hike and the slow nature walk. It is the 3 to 5 mile SHORT HIKE. The standard for short hikes was set mainly by my Wednesday hiking friends. The "short-of-time" needed to be back before the kids got home from school. The "short-of-breath" rejected the more steep and strenuous trails. But they also wanted the benefits, just described, of both serious, invigorating hikes and relaxing nature walks. The resulting short hikes described in this book represent a wide sampling of places which can be enjoyed in a few hours.

Why hike? Walking is a best exercise for cardiovascular health. It is less stressful on the feet and legs, non-competitive and self-paced. The vegetation of the forest releases oxygen, making the air much fresher. Hiking can refresh your spirits, and relax you mentally as well as physically. If the Surgeon General were to put a warning label on boots and knapsacks, it would have to read:

"WARNING: HIKING MAY BE BENEFICIAL TO YOUR HEALTH"

CHAPTER 1
FIRST STEPS
Preparation

Start at the bottom. Many of the gentle trails can be done in sensible walking shoes or good quality athletic shoes, <u>when the weather is nice</u>. But if you plan to walk on Pennsylvania trails, you can expect unforgiving rocks -- sometimes hidden under fallen leaves -- and wet underbrush, slippery mud, unpredictable ice, snow and rain. It is not fun to fall, to be wet, or cold, or injured. You will need footwear which will keep your feet dry and warm, and protected from abrasion, without causing blisters, and which will give you firm footing in all sorts of terrain.

Hiking involves the whole body, but success depends on your feet. If you think you can't afford to buy good BOOTS right now, just remember that boots are less expensive than broken bones. I recommend investing in good, 6-inch high boots with hard rubber (*Vibram*) lug soles. These boots will cushion and support your ankles. Leather boots can be waterproofed with a beeswax product (*Sno-seal*). On fabric boots, liquid silicone applied with a dauber works better. Some lightweight boots are made with waterproof breathable fabric liners (*Goretex*). Leather boots may be more durable. Just look for the best boots you can afford that will work for you. It's worth the money to buy from an outdoor supply store where the clerks have some hiking experience and will understand your needs. A reputable store will stand by their product, refunding or exchanging until you are satisfied. Boot manufacturers will often replace boots that have not lived up to their reputation. Your boots should fit perfectly. If you are in doubt, keep looking until you find the right fit. Wear your new boots around the house for short periods until they are accustomed to your feet. Before wearing them on a trail, be sure they will not be giving you trouble. **Take good care of your boots** and they will repay you with many miles of wear. They are your ticket to adventure.

The SOCKS are just as important as the boots. They should fit neatly without bunching or rubbing seams. Dry feet will not get blisters. Wear liner socks of polypropylene to wick away moisture from the feet, and outer socks of wool to absorb the moisture and stay comfortable. If you can't tolerate wool, try a synthetic. For example, "*Thor-lo*" socks were designed by a hiker, specifically for hiking on the Appalachian Trail. Their special weave has extra padding in all the right places. These polypro blend socks are a good choice, especially for summer.

Cotton clothing can kill you! Unless there is NO chance of cold rain or snow, DON'T WEAR COTTON JEANS. America's love affair with blue jeans must be put aside when venturing into our eastern rain forests. The trouble with 100% cotton denim is that it stays wet forever. Even at 50°F. body heat is conducted away fast, and hypothermia can result. Yes, cotton is natural, but a blend with polyester will dry faster and be much safer. Don't worry, polyester is not endangered yet. Choose it.

DRESS IN LAYERS. This makes you more adaptable in regulating your body temperature. On an average winter day, three layers will do: 1)polypropylene underwear for wicking; 2)wool or poly fleece sweater for insulation; 3)parka for wind and rain. You should also wear a hat. More heat is lost through the head than through any other body part. And don't forget your mittens. If your hands are stuck in your pockets when you stumble, you might land on your nose.

In cold weather you should wear wool or synthetics. Polyester fleece, which I call "fuzzy wear", is my favorite for its cuddlyness. Wool also retains its insulating properties even when wet, which makes it far superior to cotton for warmth. You can get wet from precipitation, condensation, or perspiration. Be prepared for some or all of the above to happen, even on a cold day when you are doing something strenuous, like climbing a hill.

In warm weather, lightweight, light colored, and absorbent cotton clothing can be worn. But long pants and sleeves are still usually preferable. Although shorts are cool, you should wear them **only** if you know that the trail is gentle and open, and you won't have to bushwhack through briars, poison ivy, or stinging nettles, and can risk attack by bees, ticks, mosquitos, and sunburn. You may be glad to have one light layer between you and the environment. Insect repellent and sunscreen and wide-brimmed hats, should also be part of your summer wardrobe.

In wet weather you will want something WATERPROOF. If you can not afford a breathable *Goretex* parka, at least take along a poncho made of coated nylon or plastic -- or an umbrella. Though some may snicker at these city items in the woods, they will work just as well there as in town. I don't recommend challenging a lightning storm or a 100 year flood, but with dry boots and a raincoat, a threat of drizzle should not deter you. Many small critters are more active when the woods are wet. For example, the red eft, a land stage of the familiar red-spotted salamander, is usually seen only after a rain. These outrageously orange efts can really brighten a dreary day.

What's in the pack? Even if you're going only on a short hike, you should PACK A SMALL KNAPSACK with essentials and emergency items. Use common sense. A cell phone, if available, might become a life line in some circumstances. Carry some antihistamine (*Benadryl*) to stop dangerous allergic reactions to bee stings; some antiseptic and bandaids, or moleskin for blisters; a pocket knife; matches; compass.

IMPORTANT! Always Leave a plan!
Before you go out, let someone know where you plan to hike. Then stay with the plan, so they know where to look for you.

It is not fun to be lost, or hungry or thirsty. Take a map of the trail, water and some food. An easy trail snack to carry in your pack is "GORP" -- good old raisins and peanuts. An apple at eleven is a great energy booster. A simple sandwich will seem like a banquet if you enjoy it at that lunch log at the vista.

You might also want to bring a camera, binoculars, and field guides, or a "sit-upon" --a large plastic bag works as a seat while you are resting or eating. It can also be used as an emergency raincoat, or even as a garbage bag. The wilderness ethic says, "Take only photographs," but if you find some slob's litter out there, it is OK to pack it out.

Lean on me. If the trail is very rough or steep, or involves crossing streams on stepping stones, a HIKING STICK can be a great help. Choose a light but sturdy stick. It should have a comfortable grip, and stand about as high as your shoulder. A cross-country ski pole works fine. A shorter stick is not as good, as it will force you to lean too far forward, just when you should be balanced in a more upright position. A good sturdy hiking stick can become a steady friend and turn an aging two-legged hiker with weak knees into a much more secure "tripod". They are not for everyone, but some folks swear by them.

Learn how to "walk in the woods". Forget your "sidewalk strut". Learn how and where to place your feet to avoid falls. Walk with slightly bent knees. Lift your leg from the hip. Plant your foot, not just your heel, in front of you. Maintain good posture and balance. Like everything else, it may take some practice. Soon you'll be as sure-footed as a deer.

Now, do you have everything? Of course not, but you won't find out what is forgotten until you need it. Don't worry.
Life is too SHORT.

Attitude. Remember that hiking is fun. These hikes are arranged in such a way that if there is any significant uphill, it is met with early in the hike while you are fresh. The trick is to walk until you are "half-tired", and then return.

The hikes in this book are mainly on public lands -- local or state parks, forests and natural areas. Don't cross posted private land without the owner's permission.

Respecting property rights also includes that of other creatures. When you are in the woods, you are in the home of many living things. You should behave as a well-mannered guest. Be quiet and considerate. Practice low-impact hiking, so that all may enjoy the beauty of the woods.

Don't be short-changed. Hiking is not just covering ground; it is what you see and hear and feel. The more you learn about things -- what they are, how they function and interrelate with other things -- the more you will see and enjoy. Field guides, available in most bookstores, will help you to identify wildflowers, birds, edible plants, trees, ferns, rocks or whatever particular parts of nature most fascinate you. Environmental education courses are often available at the University or the High School. Shaver's Creek Environmental Center at Stone Valley Recreation Area offers outdoor learning fun for all ages. And a new Nature Center is being developed at Millbrook Marsh , too. (See Chapters 4 and 15.)

A hike is not a destination; it is a journey. Long or short, to hike is to enjoy the world. If a hike turns out to be longer than you intended, think of it as "stretching your capabilities." You have seen something new, thought fresh thoughts, met a new friend, seen a new tree or bird or flower; and your muscles may remind you that you have DONE something. **Take a short nap.**

CHAPTER 2
WALNUT SPRINGS and LEDERER
Wilderness in Town

Summary: 2 to 3 miles; 1 to 2 hours. Comfortable walking shoes are adequate for this easy walk through two natural parks in State College. Smaller side paths are good places to see birds and plants.

Features: Walnut Springs Park is a blend of the wild and the domesticated. Cultivated species of plants mix with natives. You are in a city with houses nearby; and yet, lush green growth surrounds you; a curious rabbit hops across your path; a squirrel does aerial stunts overhead; and birds are proclaiming that this is their territory. The invading crown vetch and honeysuckle bushes mingle with numerous wildflowers. Watercress grows near the spring. A few ancient oaks tower over the tiny streamlet.

History: The 19.4-acre park was acquired by the borough of State College in the early 1970's, using Project 70 funds. Originally intended only as a stormwater drainage way, it soon became apparent that there were other ecological values. At the behest of local residents, the park was left as natural as possible. Many groups cooperated in the design and building of the paths and bridges. The overall landscape design was by Mother Nature. The land in both parks is owned by the borough of State College and administered by Centre Region Parks and Recreation Dept.

In the early 1990's, the park had problems. 1.)There was no access for the equipment needed to do maintenance work on the sewer line. 2.)Increased stormwater runoff volumes had inundated the natural springs in the park, causing siltation and erosion. 3.)Native species were being overwhelmed by undesirables such as multiflora rose, honeysuckle, privet, and prolific walnut trees. In the fall of 1993 a program was begun to improve water quality, while keeping Walnut Springs as natural as possible. The Main

Path was surfaced with a fine cinder/gravel, smooth enough for wheeled vehicles -- bicycles, baby carriages and wheel chairs as well as maintenance vehicles. A small stormwater retention dam was built to slow runoff, allow silt to settle, and control erosion. A diversion channel was created to keep the runoff away from the westside spring. To help naturalize the vegetation, some privet, honeysuckle and multiflora rose was replaced with native species. Recently a new footbridge and a bird blind were built by CRPR staff with materials provided by State College Borough.

Other maps: State College Street Map; Purple Lizard Recreation Maps of State College; USGS topo/State College quad.

Getting there: From E. College Ave./ PA 26 north (*oneway, use Beaver Ave. going east*) it is 1 mile to University Drive. Turn right, go 1/2 mile to the next light; turn left into Park area. Walnut Springs Park is located off Walnut Springs Lane, the extension of Easterly Parkway northeast of University Drive. You can park on the street, at Walnut Springs, but it is better to use the parking lot in nearby Lederer Park, found just to the south on University Drive.

Hike description: Start from **Lederer Park**, where you will find comforts -- parking, picnic shelters, and portable toilets. Begin your walk on the fine gravel path of Arboretum Loop on the park's west side, entering the *W. James "Jim" Evans Memorial Oak Arboretum.* On the southwest side in a small grove with a benchseat, a large stone holds a plaque commemorating the late Jim Evans, State College Borough Arborist from 1975 to 1988.

Savor the open knoll, and stroll around the half-mile path, which encircles a grassy area, with native trees and shrubs in random clumps. Some spots have been seeded with wildflowers. Only the grassy center is mowed, presenting a kind of low impact landscaping. The path is gentle enough for baby strollers and wheelchairs, or for a quiet lunch hour.

MAP FOR WALNUT SPRINGS PARK

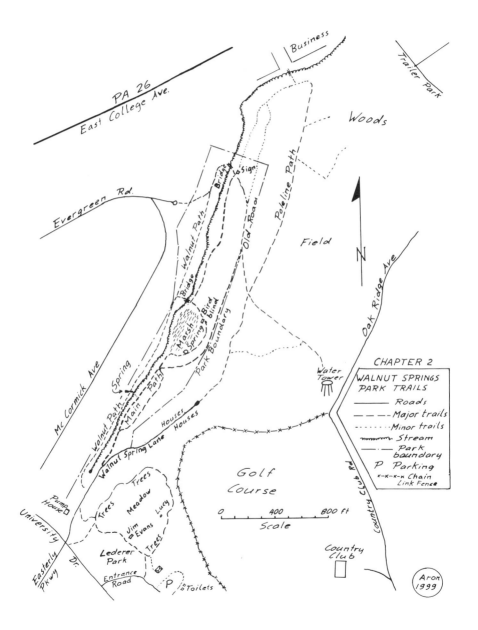

Around the knoll you may find "Remembrance Trees". Part of the Gifts-For-Parks program, which provides shade trees in this and other local parks as a means to honor special people. Birthdays, anniversaries, personal success, weddings, memorializing a loved one, or community contributions are a few occasions which may be marked with a Remembrance Tree. From 1994 through 1998, 81 new trees were planted. A brochure with details of the program is available by calling (814)-231-3071.

As you stroll around the half-mile loop, look for "*Lucy*". In a wooded nook on the northeast side there stands a small statue of Lucy C. Lederer, whose generosity helped to establish the park. It was sculpted by her son Eugene Lederer. On a pedestal, the small figure in sturdy walking shoes, holding a hiking stick, stands about 3 feet tall. (I am told that this is NOT actually life size.)

A side trail from the west side of Arboretum Loop will bring you down to Walnut Springs Lane near Walnut Springs Park.

Walnut Springs Park is 1 mile long and about 1/8 to 1/4 mile wide. Three parallel major paths run SW to NE along most of its length -- the Walnut Path on the left bank of the streamlet, the Main Path running through the center, and a broad path near the boundary, above to the right (east).

Coming down from Lederer Park, turn right onto Walnut Springs Lane. In about 100 feet look across the street to the Walnut Path. The unmarked, mowed path begins just above the large culvert which brings stormwater from Easterly Parkway into the small retention basin in the park. About 300 feet farther along the street you can see the Main Path entrance to Walnut Springs Park. Look near the yellow fire hydrant at the curve of Walnut Springs Lane. You will be returning that way.

Begin your walk on the Walnut Path. Winding through small trees and shrubs along the left bank of the streamlet, it is a favorite haunt of warblers in the springtime. You pass a major spring emerging from the hillside on the west, and soon after that there is a short path to the right connecting back to the Main Path via a major new footbridge which replaces the former twin bridges.

Continue on Walnut Path to its end below the cul-de-sac of Evergreen Road. Turn right, cross the stream on a footbridge, and join the Main Path at its intersection with the eastside "boundary path", where a sign identifies the northern end of the park. The wide "boundary path" goes up one level to the east and parallels the Main Path back towards the entrance. Unofficial trails continue beyond the park land and emerge on PA 26, and in other areas.

If this is your first walk in Walnut Springs Park, you should turn right at the intersection, and head back (SW) along the Main Path. Near the new footbridge the path turns up one level to the left (east). There you will find a new structure -- a bird blind -- overlooking the small cattail wetland. This 3-sided wooden shed offers shelter from a sudden storm, as well as a vantage point for observing birds in the marsh. (One personal complaint: the low window is too low, and the high window is too high for persons who are 4'9", although admittedly we are a small minority.)

Continuing along your path, you soon reach the old stone-lined spring. The path turns down to the right (west) into a pleasant area with a pair of resting benches near the spring. You can sit here and contemplate the flowing water, the birds, or the red winterberry bush. Only a few years ago this spring was overgrown and hidden from view. Now it has been improved for the enjoyment of all.

Turn left (SW) along the stream, and Follow the Main Path back to Walnut Springs Lane. Retrace your steps back to your car.

CHAPTER 3
MOUNT NITTANY
The Fuji of Happy Valley

Summary: Option #1: 1 mile; 1 hour walking time; steep half-mile climb to the 2000 ft. ridgetop for a view, and return the same way.

Option #2: Add a 3 or 5 mile loop walk on top of the mountain; total distance 4 or 6 miles. Add stops for breathing, eating, and looking. Plan on a 3 to 4 hour trip.

Location: 3 miles east of State College. Start from PA 26N.

Features: Mt. Nittany, the "sacred" mountain for which the Penn State Nittany Lion sports teams are named, may be the most frequently climbed mountain in the area, and the trail to the top is heavily used. The land on top belongs to the Lion's Paw Association of Penn State Alumni, and the Mount Nittany Conservancy, who hope to preserve its natural state for the enjoyment of many future generations of Penn Staters. On a clear day there is a fine view of State College from the vista, which has recently been named *Mike Lynch Overlook*. If you have not climbed THE mountain, it is about time you did.

History: 525 acres on top was purchased in 1945 by Penn State's Lions Paw Alumni Association. An additional 300 acres has been acquired by Mount Nittany Conservancy since 1981. The goal is to manage all the mountain top land above 1300 feet elevation, to protect it from commercial development, and retain public access to this treasured natural landmark. You can support this effort by joining Mount Nittany Conservancy. Contact them at PO Box 296, State College, PA 16804. The cost is $25.

The original switchback trail was constructed by Penn State Outing Club in 1978. Heavy use and misuse has always taken its toll on the mountain -- erosion, trash, stolen signs, and fire damage.

MAP FOR MOUNT NITTANY

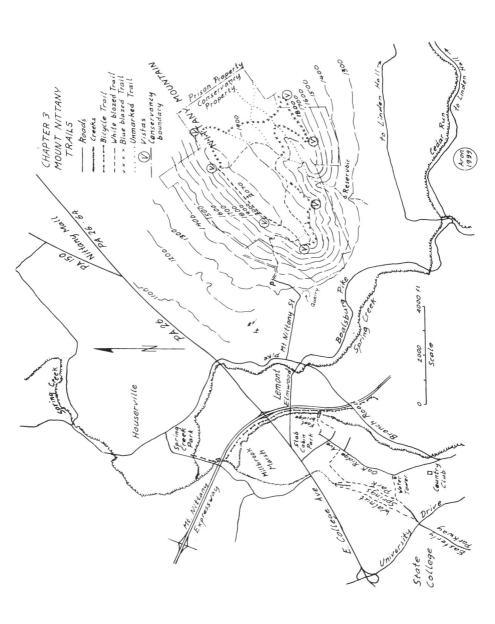

In 1997 and 1998, Tom Smyth, a retired professor of entomology and biophysics at Penn State, and former advisor to PSOC, began spending several days a week working on Mount Nittany, coordinating the creation and maintenance of the Conservancy's trails. He had some help from High School groups, PSU Alumni, and other volunteers on United Way's Day of caring in 1998, but the Lion's share of the work was done by "Mount Nittany Man", as the newspaper dubbed him. This sustained effort by Tom Smyth, (spelled with a "y" and pronounced with a "smile"), has made the climb somewhat easier for us "pilgrims".

At least one additional switchback has been added, to make the climb less steep; water bars have been installed to curb erosion. The old white-blazed trails have been refurbished, and about 3 miles of new blue-blazed trail have been added to the mountain top since 1997. Four new vistas have been opened, including three on the south side, offering views of Boalsburg and Mount Nittany Middle School; and one on the north side above Rockview State Prison, from which you can see Bald Eagle Mountain and the Allegheny Plateau beyond. Thanks mainly to the work of Tom Smyth, we have vistas we haven't evened named yet.

Other maps: State College Street Map; Purple Lizard Recreation Maps; USGS/ State College quad; PA Gazetteer, pg. 62.

Getting there: To drive to the Mt. Nittany hike, take East College Ave. (PA 26 North) from State College to the traffic light at Elmwood St. just before the Mt. Nittany Expressway. Turn right and drive to the traffic light in Lemont. Turn left onto Pike Street, go 2 blocks and turn right onto Mt. Nittany Road. The street goes up several blocks before making a bend to the left and ending at a private driveway. Park on the roadside. (Parking for larger groups is available at the old rock quarry, reached by turning right instead of left at the bend of the road. Or on Sundays you can park at the Lemont P.O. and walk an extra mile up the road.)

Hike description: Where Mt. Nittany Road ends, you will see a white-blazed trail leading to the right, up the mountain. This is the White Trail, named for Harold White, a faculty advisor to Penn State Outing Club (PSOC) for many years. The first 200 feet of trail is on a rocky road. Soon the real trail forks off to the right. A sign there says "*Foot Travel Only*". Please leave all your wheeled vehicles behind. They have been very damaging to the steep trail.

For all you bonafide "short hikers" let's review our hill climbing technique. Take small, measured steps, and breathe in and out in rhythm with each step. Stop to rest if you must. Take your time. The mountain is not going anywhere. Appreciate it.

When you reach the top, a circle of stones provides a perfect spot for the quicker hikers to be waiting for you. When you have regrouped, turn right (southwest) still following the White Trail. Soon you will come to the Mike Lynch Overlook. From here you can get a perspective on State College, the University, Beaver Stadium and all of "Happy Valley". Even if the day is clouded, you have still had some good exercise. Smile and say proudly, **"I climbed Mount Nittany!"** If you are doing only the Option #1 minimum hike, rest awhile, then go back the way you came.

Option #2: To see more of the mountain, continue following the white blazes in a counterclockwise circle. In about 500 ft. reach the blue/white fork in the trail.

Take the right fork (blue blazes) if you choose the longer, 6-mile option, which has more new vistas, The new blue trails meander closer to the edge on the south side. After the last southern vista the blue trail heads straight north across the top to the "Rockview" view. Then it turns left (SW) and, in less than a half mile, rejoins the white blazes near the "birches" view. Finish your blue trip on the white blazes and go back down the mountain on the same trail you came up.

Or take the left fork (white blazes) if you choose the older, 4-mile loop. Look for trailing arbutus. The leathery leaves of this flower are often found in the middle of trails. They seem to like the relative openness and sunlight there. If some of the pale, pink to white blossoms are open (April - May), and if you can bend down, it is well worth your while to catch the delicate fragrance of this flower. Arbutus is protected. DON'T PICK IT.

After about a mile on the white trail there is a junction. The right fork leads down to a spring, which is the source of the Oak Hall water supply. The Oak Hall spring was included in the transfer of 200 additional acres of mountain land to the Mt. Nittany Conservancy in 1985. Since this is the only available drinking water for hikers on this part of the mountain, the Conservancy is justified in dubbing it "the Sacred Spring".

If you don't need water, just turn left at the junction and continue following the white blazes. The ground cover you might see, with the shiny green leaves and red berries, is teaberry, or wintergreen. If you are not sure, crush a leaf and smell it. The mint-like aroma will confirm its identity. The berries are edible, and refreshing, even if it seems a bit like swallowing chewing gum. You will also see chestnut oaks, and perhaps a few American chestnut trees, although the latter never get very large. The chestnut blight, which killed most of them early in this century, is still present.

The trail emerges on the north side of the mountain near another vista. Turn right and walk 100 yards or so to the so-called "birches" view. Here you can sit on some large boulders in a small grove of white birch trees and admire the view across the Nittany Mall, and countryside to the north. Have some lunch.

Now turn back on the White Trail and proceed along the northern edge of the mountain, through thickening stands of striped maple trees. One more vista is found along the way. When you reach the double-blazed intersection, where you first arrived on the top, turn right and retrace your steps back down the White Trail to your car.

NOTES:

• Mt. Nittany is accessible by bus. Take a CATA bus from State College. Get off in Lemont and walk up Mt. Nittany Road to the trail.

• Mt. Nittany can also be reached from State College on foot. It is about 4 or 5 miles each way. One should be ambitious and know the territory before trying this. The way leads through city streets, trails in Walnut Springs Park, Oak Ridge Avenue, Slab Cabin Park, and Elmwood Street bridge over Mt. Nittany Expressway to Lemont.

• The State College bypass was opened in 1986 and named the Mt. Nittany Expressway (and U.S. 322). It runs through the center of the Mt. Nittany map from south to north, passing under Branch Road and Elmwood Street.

• A bicycle path parallels the Expressway, beginning at Limerock Park in Dalevue (south of Branch Road) and ending at Puddintown Road near Spring Creek Park in Houserville, a distance of about 1.7 miles. Intermediate access to this path is available via a footbridge from Slab Cabin Park near Elmwood Street in Lemont. By using the bicycle path, walkers from both ends of the region can now easily reach Mt. Nittany on foot.

CHAPTER 4
MILLBROOK MARSH
Calcareous Wetland

Summary: 1 mile or two, 1 hour or so; Explore the area's newest Nature Center, and 50-acre wetland, close to the city.

Location: 2 miles northeast of State College. Start from PA 26 N.

Features: The Centre Region Council of Governments plans to build a 1000-foot boardwalk, so walking should be very easy and far less damaging to the marsh, as you scan for birds and plants. Millbrook Marsh is located in a limestone or calcareous valley. It follows that the alkaline-loving plants which thrive here will not be the same as those which you find in an acidic bog. You will not see blueberries, for example, such as you will find in Bear Meadows Natural Area. Most of the wetlands being preserved in Pennsylvania are acidic. Unspoiled calcareous marshes like this are less frequent.

History: In 1994 Penn State University offered a 12-acre farm, including a farmhouse, and barn, as the site for a new environmental education center. Owners of the adjacent marsh offered 50 acres along Slab Cabin Run and Thompson Run in College Township. Plans developed by Assoc. Prof. Robert Brooks, director of Penn State Cooperative Wetlands Center, for preservation of this valuable ecosystem, include measures to protect it from urbanizing pressures, while providing educational and recreational programs.

Centre Region Parks and Recreation began leasing the site in 1997 for a token $1 a year for 35 years. About 20 different community groups have combined their efforts for the marsh, including Centre County Historical Society, ClearWater Conservancy, State College Bird Club and Scout groups. For more information about programs offered, trail conditions, or to volunteer call CRPR (814)231-3071.

MAP FOR MILLBROOK MARSH

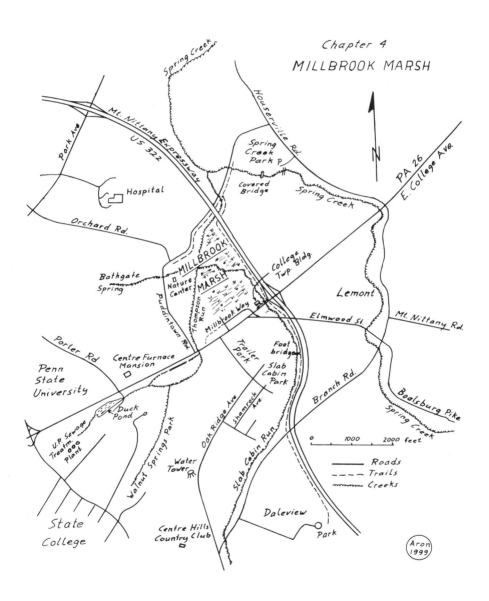

Other maps: USGS topo, State College quad; Purple Lizard Recreation Maps; PA Gazetteer page 62.

Getting there: Take East College or Beaver Avenue (PA26 northeast) less than 2 miles . Turn left (north) on Puddintown Road and within 1/2 mile look for a sign at the farm and barn on the right at the big bend of the road just before Orchard Road. A parking area and many other improvements are planned.

Hike description: Check at the barn for an updated site plan. Follow the recommended paths. Getting across the marsh will depend on where the boardwalks and bridges are. The purpose is to explore and enjoy, so a pleasant meander should work out fine. All you need are walking shoes, binoculars, and curiosity. A study conducted by Western PA Conservancy in 1995, found plants at Millbrook include swamp milkweed (*Asclepias incarnata);* spring cress (*Cardamine bulbosa),* spotted touch-me-not (*Impatiens capensis),* Virginia mountain mint (*Pycanthemum virginiana*), smooth gooseberry (*Ribes hirtellum),* common cattail (*Typha latifolia*); skunk cabbage (*Symplocarpus foetides*), and blue vervain *(Verbena hastata).* Bird life in season -- everything from tiny warblers to a great blue heron. A view of the wild marsh may include modern buildings and Mount Nittany in the background.

For a longer hike, you can circumnavigate the marsh. Use a path along Puddintown Road, under the Expressway to Spring Creek Park. Take a side trip to the Park; walk along the stream and cross Spring Creek on a covered bridge, built in 1976 by the student chapter of ASCE. (American Society of Civil Engineers). Return on the bicycle path, this time keeping left of Slab Cabin Run through the underpass and up to the bike path paralleling the Expressway. Just before the path goes under College Ave., turn up a side path to the College Township building; then follow Millbrook Way towards Puddintown Road. (You may have to walk on College Ave. briefly.) Follow Puddintown Road back to your car.

CHAPTER 5
BOALSBURG NATURE TRAIL
Short But Sweet

Summary: 1 mile; less than 1 hour walking on a mostly level trail near upper Spring Creek, down one side and back on the other. The land belongs to the Pennsylvania Military Museum.
Location: 4 miles east of State College. Start from US 322 E.

Features: Only a few steps away from human habitation, surrounded by highways and houses, this small, but rich natural area is a favorite with folks who want to get away from it all -- just for an hour. The birds, wildflowers, and soothing sounds of water have never disappointed. Each visit brings new discoveries. Be sure to bring your binoculars and field guides.

History: The trail was first cleared and blazed with red circles by the Boalsburg/ Panorama PTA in 1975. An Eagle Scout project in 1986 marked the trail with 10 numbered stop posts and printed a guide pamphlet which was available at the Military Museum. The blazes are no longer visible, and the guide pamphlet is not available, but the trail is still well used, and worth visiting. Although the footbridge has washed out, and the eastern bank is eroded and slippery in places, a new trail has been constructed farther up the slope to bypass the tricky parts. The nature trail is ripe for new scout projects. By the time you read this, things may be improved, so come out and try it.

The Shrine, or Memorial Wall area east of the museum underwent major redesign and new construction in 1997. You may want to stroll over that way and check it out for historical value. And while you are looking upstream, notice the Spring Creek "Riparian Restoration Demonstration Project". Begun by ClearWater Conservancy, the design was created by Penn State's Dept. of Landscape Architecture, and implemented through joint efforts of local business and industry, Penn State University, several PA state agencies, and conservation organizations such as Trout Unlimited. The project is attempting to restore the stream banks to a more stable, natural, erosion resistant state, and to restore habitat for native species of plants and critters in and near the stream. A kiosk poster outlines the scope of the project. For more information call project leader, Andy Otten, 814-865-7832.

Farther upstream, near the Boalsburg Pike, the old footbridge which had been built by ASCE students in 1975, was destroyed by a falling tree and washed away by the January flooding in 1996. Gert Aron, a retired Civil Engineering Professor, decided to build a replacement. Ably assisted by a neighbor, Gary McClintic, with materials provided by the Museum, and the concrete foundation work donated by Glen Hawbaker Co., he designed and built a new A-frame truss footbridge, completing it in May 1997.

Other maps: USGS topo, State College quad; Purple Lizard maps; State College street map.

Getting there: Follow South Atherton Street/ Business US 322 four miles east from State College. Turn left at the Pennsylvania Military Museum entrance. Park in the parking lot.

Hike description: After you have checked out the new additions upstream, begin your nature walk by crossing the old footbridge leading to the museum building. You may find some ducks enjoying the stream in front of the museum. A few mallards used to stay all winter, but with changes in the stream, wildlife has had to make some adjustments, too. The old dam was in disrepair, and has been removed, but the upstream dam and pond in front of the memorial wall has been restored and improved. At the museum turn left, off the sidewalk, and follow a mowed path above and behind the bushes and parallel to the stream. Pass through an open area and then back down close to the water.

MAP FOR BOALSBURG NATURE TRAIL

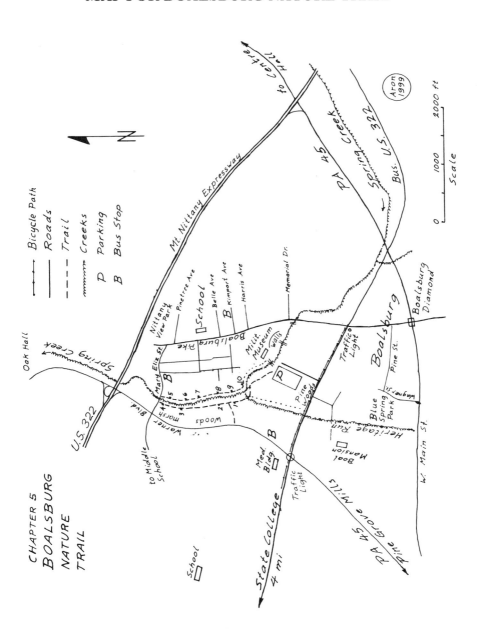

Continue following this path on the right bank of Spring Creek, heading downstream. Soon you will come to the site of a footbridge. In 1976 this was a good bridge, but recent winter storms and spring floods have washed it off its foundations.

The right bank may be a bit slippery and treacherous at times, but if you have good shoes and walk carefully, it is certainly well worth seeing. Post #10 near the bridge site, marked a large white oak tree. Following the path downstream, post #9 marked American basswood or linden trees. #8 was the outcropping of limestone. When the stream is high, you should take the new highwater trail which bypasses the difficult spot by swinging up to the right above the rocks. At its height it almost touches the private backyards, but is a much safer trail than the one at streamside.

There are many kinds of wildflowers here and farther down the path on the flood plain; especially jack-in-the-pulpit, wild columbine, hepatica, bloodroot, wood and rue anemone, spring beauties, toothwort; saxifrage, Mayapples, Solomon's seal, yellow violets, wild ginger. You may find forget-me-nots and touch-me-nots (jewelweed). Just look. Don't pick them or dig them. They won't grow in your yard. Enjoy them here and leave them for others to enjoy, too. Poison ivy is also found here.

All kinds of birds are drawn to the water. You might see sparrows, finches, juncos, a brown creeper, a yellowthroat, or just about anything that flies on feathers. Don't forget to look for critters in the water, too -- anything from tadpoles to trout.

Posts #7, 6, and 5, if they are still found, marked a shagbark hickory, a walnut tree, and American Hornbeam or ironwood tree.

The right bank trail ends at Mary Elizabeth Street. Turn left and cross the stream on the culvert. Post #4 described the crown vetch between it and the road. Post #3 described the open meadowland through which you are heading back upstream on the left bank. There is a small marshy area where cattails grow. Post #2 marked a stand of aspens. #1 marked a black walnut tree.

Just before you reach a small tributary stream called Heritage Run, there is a grove of young trees--hickory, oak, and maple--on your right. These are all less than 35 years old. This forest sprang up spontaneously after the sewer and the Route 45 spur were built. It is thick and full of surprises-- good bird habitat. It is wet enough so that horsetails, an ancient plant type, are found growing there.

Continuing on the main trail, cross Heritage Run on a small footbridge. Follow the left bank of the stream back to your car on a narrow path cutting through the so-called "weeds"--Queen Anne's lace, asters, coneflowers, wild roses, goldenrod and other such "weeds"-- which blossom in summer. Don't forget to listen. Many birds might never show themselves plainly to you, but with a little practice you will begin to recognize their songs. Birds seen and/ or heard here in late April: cedar waxwings, common yellowthroat, goldfinch, yellow warbler, cardinal, catbird. In winter you may see tracks in the snow which tell stories about rabbits, squirrels or mice. There may be tiny snow tunnels where mice travel securely in their little subways. Or a mouse trail may end abruptly with a bold imprint of large wings where an owl or hawk has had a meal.

You can extend your walk by making a side trip up along Heritage Run. Listen for all kinds of yellow birds -- goldfinch, yellowthroat, and yellow warbler. Note the many kinds of small trees which are growing spontaneously on this fertile flood plain, which has been left untilled and unmowed for a number of years.

A worn path goes all the way to the evergreen woods near the highway. Turn left and swing back to the open area and your car.

CHAPTER 6

SHINGLETOWN GAP TRAIL
The Green Tunnel

Summary: 5 mile circuit hike; 3 hours walking time. Follow a brook to its source, along an easy woods trail through a rhododendron tunnel. Return on another path. Lots of rocks and water make hiking boots a good choice for this hike.

Location: 4 miles southeast of State College. Start on US 322 E.

Features & History: Located in Harris Township, the land belongs to State College Water Authority and Rothrock State Forest. This hike is quite close to State College. In fact, in the days before the town grew so large and developed, when walking was more popular and less hazardous, Shingletown was a popular destination for college students out for a picnic. They would, of course, walk all the way from the university, crossing through fields and woods, a distance of about 4 miles from campus to the Shingletown Gap. It is still a popular place, which has been very nearly its downfall.

A small reservoir impounds water from "Roaring Run", a crystal clear brook babbling from the mountains. This high quality surface water, representing about 25% of State College Borough's water supply, was lost when giardia cysts were discovered in early 1988. State College will need an expensive filtration plant to recover this source. Giardia can be carried by most mammals, so there is no way of pinning blame on wildlife or on humans. Both have long been present in Shingletown Gap. But the late 1980's saw a marked increase in "human wild life" -- parties, bonfires, and trash; camping and human waste; hunting and deer guts; mountain bikes and erosion; littering, illegal cutting, fire danger, vandalism and disregard: in short, degradation of this traditional green space.

MAP FOR SHINGLETOWN GAP

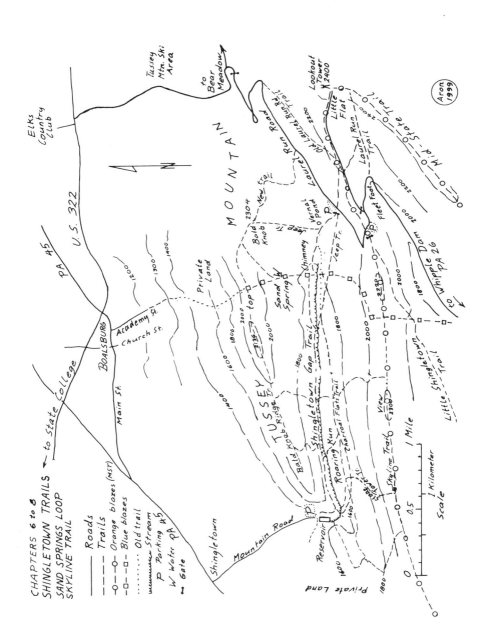

In 1989 a committee of ClearWater Conservancy called the Water Issues Task Force (WITF) took on the problem. Coordinating with the three concerned government branches: Harris Township, State College Borough Water Authority, and Rothrock State Forest District, the problem was attacked on two fronts: public education and regulation. The Bureau of Forestry made and installed signs at the trail entrance. The police stepped up patrols. The public became aware. Alternate trails, built in the early 1990's, mostly by volunteers (such as Tom Smyth, whom you met in the Mt. Nittany Chapter) have taken some of the pressure off the main trail. The area still gets heavy use, and occasional littering; but joint efforts have paid off. Either fewer people are littering, or else more people are conscientiously picking up trash. In any case by 1994 Shingletown Gap was once again a clean and pleasant green tunnel. It is up to all of us to keep it that way.

Other maps: USGS topo, State College quad; Mid State Trail map 203; Purple Lizard maps; Rothrock State Forest map; PA Gazetteer, page 62

Getting there: To get there from State College drive east on Business US 322 (South Atherton St.) to Boalsburg. Turn right on PA 45 West and drive 2 miles to Shingletown. Turn left on Mountain Road. There are only about two streets in Shingletown. You can't miss. Follow it 0.9 mile to the reservoir and park outside the chainlink fence.

Hike description: Begin the hike on the well-worn trail to the left around the fence and up past the reservoir. From April to September you may find some wildflowers here. In spring look for Canada mayflower (wild lily-of-the-valley), Solomon's seal and white violets. In May you may see patches of fringed polygala. These dainty, hot-pink flowers look like tiny orchids, though they are actually members of the milkwort family. Later in summer you can find jewelweed here, also known as touch-me-not. In summer the succulent orange flowers hang like pendant jewels, and quickly wilt if picked. In September the ripe seedpods are spring-loaded, and pop at a touch, shooting seeds in all directions.

Keep following the stream upward on the left trail fork Soon you are enclosed in a rhododendron world. When they bloom (July) it is a fantastic sight. It can also be very special when a misty day gives it a jungle-like quality, or with wet snow weighing down the leaves, or moonlight reflecting their glow.

The trail continues through more open hemlock woods. It used to cross the stream several times, but new trail construction in 1995 and 1996 now allows hikers to remain on the right bank (north side) all the way to the top. Stay to the left of the water as you go upstream, picking your way along through rhododendrons. The new parts can be narrow and tricky, but they are quite passable on foot. An unofficial trail turns left from here and climbs steeply up the rocks to join Bald Knob Ridge Trail on First Mountain, which parallels Shingletown Gap Trail on the north side of this vale.

Continue on the main Shingletown Gap Trail through a rhododendron tunnel. Soon you may notice a blazed trail across the stream to the right. This leads up to the Charcoal Flats Trail which runs parallel to the main trail, about 200 ft. higher, on the south side. You will be returning on Charcoal Flats Trail. (It is possible to short cut the circuit here for a **very** short hike.)

Near the same junction, you should see another blazed trail on the left (north), going up to join Bald Knob Ridge Trail. This one is called the 1-2 Link because it connects trail #1 with trail #2. A more strenuous hike, with some nice views, can be had by using these trails on the north side.

The short hiker continues on Shingletown Gap Trail. After passing a spring which is usually flowing across the trail, you reach an area of more open oak woods on your right. If you see some large rectangular holes which have been chiseled out of dead trees by a really large bird (15 inches tall), listen for the insulting raucous laughing call, and look for a pileated woodpecker.

If you notice a white-blazed trail to the right, with a makeshift log crossing, this would be a second chance to short circuit up to Charcoal Flats Trail.

The last stream crossing on the old main trail is deep and difficult. Just beyond it is the junction with the eastern end of Charcoal Flats Trail, blazed with blue rectangles with a white stripe. That would be the third short circuit chance. Don't bother to cross unless you want to shorten the hike. Instead turn left on the new main trail. This trail takes you through more rhododendron and mountain laurel. In half a mile you reach the dark blue-blazed Sand Spring Trail at "The Chimney". This open area was the site of a cabin at one time, which probably burned down. All that remains is the stone chimney.

Sand Spring Trail, from Academy Street in Boalsburg on your left (north) to the Mid State Trail atop Tussey Ridge on your right (south), used to be known as "Huckleberry Lane" to Boalsburgers, who came up this way to pick berries on the ridge. Several springs arise in this area. The north end of the trail, from the ridge top down to Boalsburg, is on private land and is disappearing.

Near the chimney there are a few pink lady slippers. In late May a well-timed visit could make you privileged to see one of these native wild orchids in bloom.

You may find a scarlet tanager in this relatively open, mixed hardwood forest. If you think you hear a robin with a sore throat, screaming at you to "Cheer up!", check the treetops for a red bird with black wings or his greenish-yellow mate.

The Shingletown Gap Trail continues another half mile to Laurel Run Road, passing a recently logged area. You will visit this loop in the next chapter. So, unless a shuttle car has been arranged, the Shingletown Gap short hike begins its return leg now.

From the chimney, head south on Sand Spring Trail. Cross the narrow stream on some logs. You may still find the sign for Mid State Trail at the junction with the old main Shingletown Gap Trail. The sign indicates you are 3 km from Boalsburg. Keep hiking south towards Mid State Trail for about 500 feet uphill, through boggy meadows and huckleberries. At the jeep trail crossing, turn right. You are halfway through the hike and homeward bound.

Notice this patch of woods consists mainly of multiple stump sprouts of black birch, plus a few red maples. This area was clearcut over 30 years ago and has not recovered its balance.

In half a mile you reach a boggy area. The trail veers right to rejoin the old main Shingletown Gap Trail near that difficult stream crossing, which you may recognize. A few steps to the left and you leave the main trail again for the return along Charcoal Flats Trail. Follow the blazes across some rocks and into the woods.

The trail heads west, mostly on the 1740 ft. contour level, passing through several charcoal flats. Cross trails are marked with paint blazes of other colors. Another time you can explore these, but to today you should stay on Charcoal Flats Trail. A nice spring is found soon after the first charcoal flat.

The Charcoal Flats Trail ends at a switchback of Stone Tower Trail. Follow it to the right, soon entering a steep descent on an old road through a rhododendron jungle which covers several acres. At the bottom you must cross the stream one last time on logs. Turn left; notice a beautiful splashing waterfall entering the stream from a side run. Follow the water back down to your car.

CHAPTER 7
SAND SPRING LOOP
A Sample Case

See Map for Shingletown Gap, page 35
Summary: <u>2.5 miles; allow 2 hours</u> walking and stopping time.
A variety of trails; a soft, wide jeep trail through woods, with
flowers, ferns and birds; a spring; a mild climb; a rocky knob; and a
steep but quick descent. The land is in Rothrock State Forest.

Location: 5 miles southeast of State College. Start from US 322 E.

Features & History: This is a good beginner's hike because it
offers three different types of trails in a short distance. The scenery
on this circle hike changes often. It was on this trail where I met
my first pink lady slipper and my first scarlet tanager, tasted the
spring water and added stones to the cairn on Bald Knob.

A timber harvest took place here in 1997 or 1998. Some parts
may look ugly for awhile, but it will recover. The fenced sections
which you might see, demonstrate a method of encouraging faster
forest regeneration by keeping out the over-abundant deer that
would nibble off the tender seedling trees.

Other maps: USGS topo, State College quad; Mid State Trail
map 203; Rothrock State Forest map; Purple Lizard maps.

Getting there: Take Business US 322 east (South Atherton St.)
through Boalsburg. Turn right to Tussey Mountain Ski Area.
Follow the road past new Rothrock State Forest parking lot in
Galbraith Gap. Turn right at the first junction onto Laurel Run
Road. Follow it 2 miles up. Park at a gated jeep trail on the right.
This is the east end of Shingletown Gap Trail. (See Chapter 6).

Hike description: From the gate, take the jeep trail on the right, and walk westward on a wide, gently descending path through a mixed hardwood forest, with huckleberries in the understory and various wildflowers near the trail. Look for violets and fringed polygala. After about 5 minutes, look for a vernal pond about 100 feet off the trail to your right. It is difficult to see it until you walk off the trail and cast around a bit, but it is there in springtime. The pond is very shallow, 6 to 12 inches deep, and about 50 feet wide. Check for frogs eggs or tadpoles in the water, or other discoveries.

In 0.2 mile, shortly after the pond, you pass a wide grassy trail on your right which goes steeply up the mountain. This was an access for a radio tower which used to be on Bald Knob. You will be coming down this trail on your return. Continue straight ahead.

In another 0.2 mile the trail forks again. To the left it follows the water from the springs along a narrow belt of rhododendron and evergreens. We spent a pleasant lunch time here watching an ovenbird scratching through the leaves for its meal. Another time we took shelter under the hemlocks during a passing shower. You can hop across the water and follow the old trail out to the Sand Spring Trail junction, (BM 1774 on the topo map) where you may find the Mid State Trail sign which you met in the last Chapter. Then follow the blue blazed Sand Spring Trail to the right (north), crossing the still-narrow stream on logs to "The Chimney".

Alternately, you can skip the rhododendron belt and instead keep right at the fork. You will arrive at "The Chimney" without making any stream crossings. The distance is the same either way.

There used to be a cabin here, but this chimney and the sandy-bottomed reservoir up the trail are all that's left of it. The springs are the source of the Shingletown part of State College's water supply, which they hope to recover in the future.

The pink lady slippers found in this area bloom from late May into early June. DO NOT even THINK of taking them. They are virtually impossible to transplant, as they need special conditions.

Turn right (north) on the blue-blazed Sand Spring Trail which climbs the mountain gently. Look for cinnamon fern, mayapples, and wild azalea, which blooms in late May. Listen and look for birds: scarlet tanager, brown creeper, yellow throat, towhee, ovenbird, chickadee, American redstart, perhaps a great crested flycatcher. A few years ago, when the area was infested with gypsy moth caterpillars, a black-billed cuckoo was heard here. Cuckoos are one of the few birds who like the hairy gypsy moth caterpillars. The infestation left many dead oak trees. Now the maples and other species are beginning to fill in.

The tiny, sandy-bottomed reservoir and the spring a little way above it are found about 0.1 mile up the trail from the chimney. Where the water emerges from the mountain, it is probably safe to drink, having been filtered through a few hundred feet of rocks and sand. However, since the discovery of giardia cysts in so many places, all water sources are suspect. You should always carry water (or a filter) on a hike. But in an emergency, if you must have clean water, this is the most likely place.

In about 0.3 mile, halfway up the mountain where the trail forks again, leave the blue trail and choose the unblazed but obvious trail on the right. This old moss-covered track climbs gradually on the diagonal to the northeast towards Bald Knob. It passes near a couple of old charcoal flats, where colliers burned their mounds of wood into charcoal about a century ago. One flat has white pines growing on it now. The other one is home to huckleberry and mountain laurel. Soon you reach an intersection with the blazed Bald Knob Ridge Trail; turn right and proceed to Bald Knob. A faint trail ahead leads to the north edge of the mountain, where you can get a view through the trees of Boalsburg and Mt. Nittany.

If you missed the diagonal "charcoal" trail, you can continue on the blue trail to the top. The total vertical rise is only about 300 feet. The blue blazes used to continue down the north side to Academy Street in Boalsburg. Sand Spring Trail was a side trail, access, and connector to the Mid State Trail. Now, it seems, the trail has been surrendered to "private property rights", which we must respect. But, in an emergency it is the quickest way out.

On the ridgetop follow the Bald Knob Ridge Trail east to the open rock pile which is Bald Knob, elevation 2300 feet. There used to be a radio tower on Bald Knob. You can still see some concrete foundations and the maintenance access jeep trail. Around 1971 the tower was moved over to Little Flat, the next knob to the east, which is 100 feet higher (2400) and slightly more accessible with a road and a helicopter pad. There is a cairn of stones on Bald Knob. Every hiker should add another stone to the pile, thereby making the mountain taller. Nobody loves a short mountain.

In summer you can find a few huckleberries ready to eat here. Also look for mountain columbine among the rocks. When the trees are bare, in winter, you may get a view of sorts. To the northeast you can look down on Tussey Mountain Ski slope, And you can usually see the radio tower at Little Flat to the east.

A new trail down from Bald Knob to Laurel Run Road was built in 1996. It is quite rough and rocky in places, but you can use it to complete your hike if you don't mind going the extra mile. To reach your car, turn right when you reach Laurel Run Road .

Otherwise take the old maintenance trail down from Bald Knob. It is also somewhat rocky, but will get you back quicker, as it descends quite steeply down the south side. At the bottom, turn left (east) on the trail you came in on, and return 0.2 mile to your car.

CHAPTER 8
SKYLINE TRAIL
Looking Down on Happy Valley

See Map for Shingletown Gap, page 35.

Summary: The Option #1 short hiker can see this magnificent view on a 2.8-mile, 2-hour out-and-back hike. The more enterprising Option #2 hiker can enjoy a challenging 8.3-mile, 5 to 6 hour loop hike with more views and varied terrain. For the in-between set, several other hike options from this spot are possible, and are mentioned here briefly. They range from 3 or 4 mile shuttle hikes to 5 or 10 mile loops.

Location: 6 miles southeast of State College. Start from US 322 E.

Features & History: How does the hawk feel as it soars above the ridges? What does Happy Valley look like from up there? Thanks to a piece of Mid State Trail on Tussey Mountain, completed in November 1982 by Penn State Outing Club's Hiking Division, we can get a birdseye view of State College and even look down on Mount Nittany from a new perspective.

Pick a crystal clear day when visibility is fine -- a day when you can break away from all other obligations for a few hours. A pilgrimage to this view on such a day is indeed a rare privilege, and a treat for the eyes and the spirit. Be sure to bring your lenses -- binoculars and cameras. The trail is rough and rocky. Wear sturdy boots and carry a walking stick for balance.

Other maps: USGS topo, State College, and McAlevy's Fort quads; Rothrock State Forest map; Mid State Trail map 203; and Purple Lizard Recreation map.

Getting there: To get to Skyline Trail: from US 322, six miles east of State College turn onto Bear Meadows Road and drive past

Tussey Mountain Ski Area. At the first junction, turn right and follow Laurel Run Road about 2.5 miles to the crest of the ridge. Park near the gated Little Shingletown Roadtrail on the right, where the orange-blazed Mid State Trail crosses Laurel Run Road. Don't block the fire emergency gate!

Hike description: Walk around the gate and begin following the orange blazes westward slightly uphill. In 0.2 mile the Mid State Trail leaves Little Shingletown Roadtrail. Keep to the right following the orange blazes along the ridge top. Shortly after passing a primitive campsite in the gum grove (black gum or tupelo trees), you cross the blue-blazed Sand Spring Trail. The sign says it is 4 km to Boalsburg. Continue straight ahead.

The trail gets rougher, but don't give up. It is worth the trip. Soon you will begin to get glimpses of Happy Valley through the trees. After passing an area of hemlock trees which grace the north edge of the mountain, at 2.26 km (about 1.4 miles) from the start you will find the "View". A sign on a tree points to the obvious. A scree slope provides a natural overlook, further improved by selective clearing. This is the most spectacular and comprehensive view of the town, the University, and the entire region to be found around here ---short of flying. Notice the true shape of Mt. Nittany and the Oak Hall gap as seen from this new angle. From the far left of the overlook, you can see to the right as far east as Centre Hall.

After looking over the overlook, Option #1 minimum hikers turn around and retrace your steps to the car.

Option #2 challenge hikers should continue west from the "View", along the ridge. As you hike you may catch more glimpses of State College to the right (north) through the trees. Caution: STOP your feet BEFORE you look. There is a nice view from "The Roman Tower", a square stone platform about 8' by 8' of unknown origin, which stands at the northern edge of the ridge, directly above

Shingletown Gap. The "tower" is not readily visible from the MST, but can be reached by following a side loop trail to the right (north) at 2.2 miles. The Tower is a popular lunch stop. Short hikers may opt to turn back here, making a 4-mile out-and-back hike.

Just west of the "Roman Tower", a side trail heads north, steeply down into Shingletown Gap. This trail (Stone Tower Trail) or the next one half a mile farther west (Deer Path) can be used to make a 3- to 5-mile shuttle hike, if you have a car waiting at Shingletown Gap. Be advised that these trails are very rocky, and can be treacherous, especially when covered with fallen leaves. Another possibility for the really intrepid hiker is to devise a 5- to 10- mile strenuous circuit hike using various trails climbing in and out of the Shingletown Gap system. You are on your own.

Back to the Option #2 hiker on the ridge: At 2.35 miles you begin crossing the narrow "knife edge". At 2.9 and 3.3 miles you'll find two wilder views to the south, overlooking Hubler Gap and across to Big Flat and Greenlee Mountain.

At 3.9 miles from the start you reach Musser Trail at the powerline swath where it crosses the ridge above Musser Gap. Some good views may be had from here, too. Ahead the ridge trail continues and soon becomes the blue-blazed Jackson Trail. It is another 3.5 rough miles to PA 26 at the Jo Hays Vista above Pine Grove Mills. With a second car spotted there, this could become a shuttle hike of 7.4 miles; but unless you really like rocky ridges, it is not recommended.

To complete the option #2 loop you can turn left and descend steeply on the Musser Trail, 0.6 mile down to Pine Swamp Road. Turn left and go another 0.6 mile, then turn left again onto Little Shingletown Road. Begin the gradual but steadily uphill walk, 3.2 miles on a grassy jeep trail back to your car.

Bonus:

LITTLE SHINGLETOWN DOWNHILL WALK

Another possible easy hike, enjoyed by the Senior Citizens Hiking Group, is the 3.2-mile DOWNHILL walk on Little Shingletown Roadtrail. Use a Rothrock State Forest map to find the roads. First spot a car at the bottom, off Pine Swamp Road. Then use Laurel Run Road to drive shuttle to the top, where you parked for the Skyline Trail. Allow 1.5 to 2 hours to walk back down on this easy old road. Black birch trees are found along Little Shingletown Road. Break a twig and smell the wintergreen flavor. Little Shingletown is still a fire emergency access road for the Bureau of Forestry. If you find campfire rings or trash blocking the road, you can help by dismantling the rings and removing the trash. Be alert for sudden silent bicycles rushing along this trail. Apart from that, Little Shingletown trail is very gentle. The hazards are few and the joys are many.

CHAPTER 9
BIG HOLLOW
Arboretum in Progress

Summary: 2 miles, 1 hour; or 4 miles, 2 hours, round trip walk from University Park campus; through a valley on a railroad grade from Sunset Park to Toftrees. Return on alternate trails.

Location: 1 mile north of State College. Start from US 322 W.

Features: Designated Arboretum land on the University's master plan, Big Hollow has potential to become a significant scientific and aesthetic resource. The topo map still shows blue "streams" flowing through this valley, but you may see only grass flowing through the broad vale. The streams are all underground, having been swallowed long ago by the limestone underlying the area. The University draws water from several well sites along Big Hollow and Fox Hollow. Along the old Bellefonte Central railroad grade and the broad hollow paralleling it, you will find moist meadows, groves of trees, shrubs and flowers. Big Hollow holds some rare plants and a nice, two-centuries old, oak woodlot.

Whether or not you will see a **"Penn State Arboretum"**, will depend on complex factors, but we have high hopes that it will happen within the next few years. The final draft of the plan was completed in February 1999. The Arboretum is in the University Master Plan, and is in high favor. The main stumbling block might be funding. The budget will be phased in over a 10-year period. Arboretums are very expensive, so substantial public support will be needed and greatly appreciated. You can help make it happen by sending **donations to the University, allocated for the Arboretum Project**. (allocation code PXXUA) For further information contact Prof. Kim Steiner at 814-865-9351.

MAP FOR BIG HOLLOW

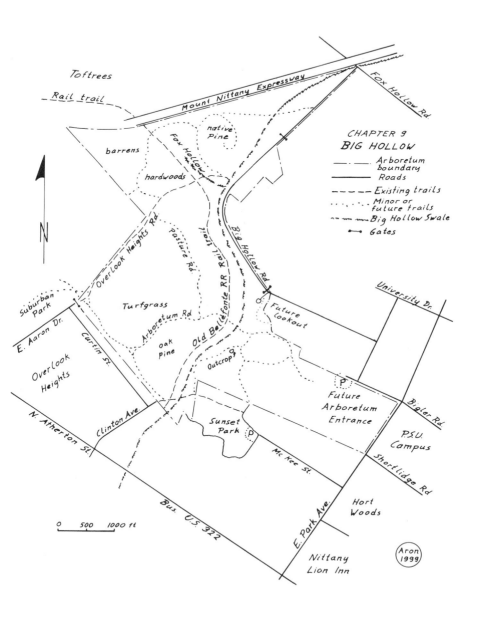

History: Since 1907 there have been repeated efforts to establish an arboretum on the University Park campus. At first it was to be in "Hort Woods" and around the current Nittany Lion Inn. In 1914 some land (25 acres) was set aside in what is now the northeast corner of the golf course. A landscape plan was made in 1924 but dropped in 1925. Again in 1927 an arboretum was proposed, this time it was to be at Thompson Spring (near College Ave. between University Drive and Porter Road) in an area now known as "the Duck Pond". The plan was approved by the Trustees and drew wide support, but fell victim to a lack of funding during the Great Depression of the 1930's.

The idea languished for nearly 35 years. Then in 1972 and 1973 a committee was appointed and a tract of 320 acres of Big Hollow lands was identified and reserved for an arboretum. A master plan was developed in 1976 and a fund-raising effort was begun. But the project never received the priority it should have had, and again it languished for another 15 years.

In 1995 a Penn State Arboretum Task Force, chaired by Kim C. Steiner, Professor of Forest Biology, proposed that a 370-acre tract (the Big Hollow lands plus the newly-acquired Mitchell tract) be developed as an arboretum. A plan, begun in 1996 by Sasaki Associates, Inc. of Watertown, MA, has undergone several revisions, but in 1999 the final draft was completed. Perhaps in 2000, work will begin on relocating the Turf Grass Research Center, and the Flower Trial Gardens, and building a visitor center, greenhouses, etc. The vision of the Arboretum Task Force includes such components as the Public Green, Theme Gardens, and Ecosystem/ Habitat Zones. It will be an outdoor classroom which will benefit every college in the University, as well as providing education and enjoyment to the general public.

I repeat: **Public support will be needed. Send donations to the University, allocated for the <u>Arboretum Project</u>**. For further information contact Prof. Kim Steiner at 814-865-9351.

Other maps:USGS, State College and Julian quads; Purple Lizard Recreation Maps of State College; Penn State Campus map.

Getting there: Starting from Business US 322 West (North Atherton St.) just north of the University, turn right at Nittany Lion Inn onto E. Park Ave. Drive three blocks and turn left (north) on McKee St. Drive five blocks to the end, and park at Sunset Park.

*If the 21st century has arrived by the time you read this, and the creation of Penn State Arboretum has begun, **the new "Arrival Area/** Education Center", and parking for 75 cars, **will be just off of Bigler Road** to the north of Park Ave. Drive 6 blocks from North Atherton St. or about 2 miles west from the Expressway on Park Ave. The plan for the "arrival" block includes a pond and event lawn, flower trial gardens, demonstration specialty gardens, greenhouses and conservatory, historic Parterre Gardens, and an outdoor amphitheater. Trails will lead out from here to all parts of the Arboretum. The future looks grand. But for the time being we will enter the Big Hollow area from Sunset Park*

Hike description: Begin hiking down the paved bicycle path, which curves downhill into Big Hollow. This short bike path is only 0.36 mile long and connects to Clinton Ave. in Overlook Heights. Alternately you can follow a dirt path which cuts diagonally to the right through the woods (mature oak, pine, hickory).

At the bottom of the hill turn right and look for a way up onto the old railroad grade which runs through this valley on the "left bank" of the invisible stream. This old Bellefonte Central rail trail may someday be developed as a hike/ bike trail. As of this writing it is dirt-surfaced, and kept open only by popular use. It heads north and west, reaching Toftrees residential area in about 2 miles. You can stay on it the whole way, or you can simply use it as an anchor, or mainline trail. There are plenty of reasons to leave the rail grade on side expeditions. You can always find it again if you need to re-orient yourself.

If you walk on the narrow, worn footway through the bottom of the Hollow, you can see that the rounded valley has been carved by water. Although the water is underground, this is a major drainway, and flood plain. In a really big storm you might still see some water flowing in Big Hollow. *In about 1/4 mile look for a limestone outcrop on the right, where an interpretive area is planned.*

In about 1/2 mile, at an old fence, a gravel road (*Arboretum Road)* goes up to the right. You can opt to hike up and get onto Big Hollow Road, a gated, paved University road, which parallels your trail at this point. *A future lookout is planned near here. To the left (west), Arboretum Road will lead up to the future Turf Grass Research Facility*

In the hollow you pass a few sheds at water well sites. After 1 mile you reach a crossroad. The gravel extension of East Aaron Drive, *called Overlook Heights Road,* comes in from the left and joins Big Hollow Road, at "the bend". Both the hollow and the road bend 90-degrees to the right and head out 1 short mile to Fox Hollow Road at a Mt. Nittany Expressway overpass. The drainway of Big Hollow continues eastward until it enters Spring Creek along Rock Road *near the proposed new I-99 crossing.* The "burn site", which was used to train fire fighters, is also at "the bend". In 1998/99 it was found to contain some PCE-contaminated soil, probably dating from the 1960's and '70s. The drinking water was not affected, but safety regulations necessitated an expensive clean-up.

Your hike continues north and west on the rail grade, or on other roads or trails leading up the Fox Hollow drainway, which comes in to "the bend" from Toftrees.

About 1/4 mile after passing "the bend" the trail goes under the Expressway, and continues parallel to it until you reach the Toftrees area. Lots of unofficial trails branch off around Toftrees, which you can explore on your own. *A Penn State retirement village is being planned for that area. Active seniors will make good use of this trail, and the Arboretum.*

On the return hike, if you have followed the railgrade up to now, you may want to vary it. Once you are back on the University side of the Expressway underpass, look for a side trail or crossroad (*future: Barrens Road*). To the west it will go through a *barrens plant community* and a *northern forest.* To the left (east) it goes through a *pine plantation*, and to a hilltop of *native pine -- pitch, white and Virginia pine.*

Another trail or dirt road near a well site, will take you back to "the bend". The area is very small. You won't get lost if you pay attention.

When you are happily half-tired, you can take Big Hollow Road, the rail trail, or any other trail you find heading from "the bend" back up Big Hollow to find your car.

CHAPTER 10
THE BARRENS
Fertile Ground for Hiking

Summary: <u>1 to 5 miles, 1 to 3 hours</u>. Plan your own hike on flat to moderately rising Gamelands trails; or <u>4 miles, 2 hours</u> to do the Greenbriar Loop, a popular x-c ski route.

Location: 1 to 4 miles west of State College. Start on US 322 W.

Features: "The Barrens" is a large area of gently rolling forest land, 1200 to 1400 feet in elevation. The land is occupied mainly by the PA Game Commission's Gamelands #176. Featuring 6500 acres of woodlands, it is full of wildlife and a wide variety of plants and birds. Find tracks of deer, rabbit, grouse, turkey, fox, bear, and x-c skiers. After a fresh snow, when the stillness is padded with fluff-covered branches, this area will seem like an ice cream sundae, just waiting to be tasted. A variety of hikes can be planned on easy, gamelands trails. Visit Scotia ghost town; or Chimney Rock. See birds at Scotia Pond. Cross-country ski on a network of trails with reasonable grades. Be prepared with map and compass; food and water; binoculars and guidebooks. Come back often.

History: "Barrens" is a misnomer. Although corn would not grow in the red acid clay, it is far from barren. Wild plants cover every inch. Wild game thrives. It is barren only of people. Once covered by dense pine forests, a mining boom in the 1880's brought several towns, sawmills, charcoal furnaces, and iron mines to the area; which in turn brought a huge demand for wood. The rapid deforestation and devastating forest fires helped to bring overall changes in the weather, and even the soil, which left stunted, scraggly oaks and scrawny pitch pines and aspens instead of the former dense forest canopy. Data collected from 1977 to 1997 by Jay Schlegel, at PSU Weather Station, indicate that the Barrens are one of the coldest places in the state. Sub-freezing temperatures have been recorded in every month of the year.

MAP FOR THE BARRENS

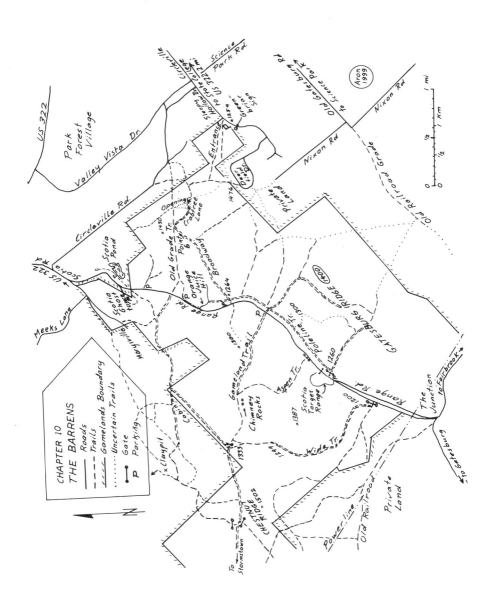

An iron mining town of 450 people, called Forest City, was begun in 1882. It was later named "Scotia", after Scotland, the homeland of Andrew Carnegie, who planned to turn it into the "Model Iron City of Pennsylvania". But the dream died. When operating costs became too great, Scotia was sold to the Bellefonte Furnace Co. in 1898 and came to a final standstill in 1911.

Other maps: USGS topo map, Julian quad; Penn State Outing Club map 104/105 (1983); KTA's *Pennsylvania Hiking Trails*, 12th ed., 1998; PGC Sportsmen's map; Purple Lizard Recreation map.

Getting there: Access can be on the north from Scotia Road via Range Road; on the west from Stormstown; or on the south from Whitehall Road, via Tadpole, Gatesburg and Range Roads. The only access which gets you directly onto gamelands from a paved, plowed road is on the east from Sleepy Hollow Drive.

The Barrens is best visited in winter and in spring, when other places are less accessible. Many gamelands trails are suitable for X-C skiing and have been explored by Penn State Outing Club X-C Ski Division. The wide swath trails may be **hot** in summer. If possible, choose a narrower path through woods then. Always carry a map, compass, and drinking water. Gamelands are busiest in hunting seasons, since they are managed primarily for game animals. Although this is changing to meet the needs of other recreationists, the Game Commission does not assume responsibility for trail conditions. For safety and courtesy, the skier or hiker should choose another place during hunting seasons, or hike on Sundays when no hunting is allowed.

Hike description: To visit Scotia Pond and the ghost town, drive west 5 miles on US 322. At the northern end of the Mt. Nittany Expressway, turn left on Scotia Road and drive 0.8 mile. Turn left onto Range Road, near a power substation. A small sign says "Scotia Range 3 miles". This 4-mile long gravel road traverses the gamelands from north to south, and passes the Scotia Target Range. However, the Game Commission has now closed this road in the middle in order to discourage through traffic.

From Scotia Road Drive 0.3 mile to the first parking spot on the left. This gives access to an old railroad grade trail on an embankment which parallels Range Road for 0.3 mile, and provides an easy walk and access for viewing Scotia Pond, hidden behind it.

Walk along the grade and look out across this large pond, strewn with water lilies; hear the bullfrog croak and the catbird sing. Watch the swallows swoop across the water. Bring your field guides, and identify plants and birds at this hidden pond. Find spotted knapweed, goldenrod, daisies, staghorn sumac, white birch, blackberries. Although the barrens are dotted with small, standing ponds, there is little or no water moving above ground here.

Next, walk or drive another 0.1 mile along the Road to the ghost town of Scotia. Turn off Range Road to the right. Behind the gate is an open area with dirt paths going off in three directions. You will be doing a 20 minute loop in a clockwise direction. Begin on the leftmost path. Almost immediately the path splits. Keep left again heading southwest. The path is somewhat overgrown. Follow the main footway, but make short side trips to look for ghost town ruins. After a short distance, back in the woods to the right you see a concrete structure in a state of decay. It may be the ruins of part of the ore washer building; or it may date only from the 1940's when Scotia was reopened briefly during World War II. Look around for other foundations and ruins of unknown origin, scattered and mostly lost in the woods. Return to the main path and continue, bearing right in a clockwise circle through a clearing, and along an easy old road arching northeast back to the split and the open area near the gate.

A second short walk from this spot can be made on the path which heads north. It takes you through an unreal landscape of reddish piles of mine tailings to a large pond. This one has unnatural blue-green water and seems fairly lifeless. Contrast this one with Scotia Pond. Assorted other trails can take you around this pond on adventurous explorations, if you like. Just be sure you take notice of compass direction and landmarks. **If you tend to get lost easily, don't try these walks alone.**

Study the map, and choose a circle or an out-and-back hike of any length you prefer. One unusual landmark is a rock formation called Chimney Rock. Located about a mile north of Scotia Target Range, an interesting, weathered rock juts from the top of a knoll, looking like a ruined fortress, or a breaching submarine. Vines, ferns, and wildflowers cover its lower slopes -- Virginia creeper, poison ivy (be careful), walking fern, hepatica, wood anemone, and pussytoes. Five large cucumber trees, a native magnolia, grow like bold sentinels from the top of the rock.

GREENBRIAR LOOP: 4 miles. 2 hours, a favorite x-c ski trail. Near the Greenbriar residential section, a gamelands appendage reaches invitingly towards State College. From North Atherton Street (Business Route 322), drive 2 miles west on W. Clinton Ave. or Circleville Road. The trailhead is on Sleepy Hollow Drive, half a mile west of the 4-way stop at the intersection of Science Park Road, Valley Vista Drive, and Circleville Road. Park near the large stone sign that says "Greenbriar". The trail you want is just east of the sign. Note the boundary markers for the gamelands -- red ovals with white lettering, plus white blazes on trees.

Soon after entering the woods take the right fork. Now you are on the Entrance Trail which will take you up through the narrow neck of the "appendage" to the main body of the gamelands. From Greenbriar it is about a 200 ft. rise to the top of Gatesburg Ridge (1400 ft. elevation).

Near the top, ignore the first path to your left which leads to a private backyard. But soon afterwards turn left at the T intersection to avoid leaving gamelands.

Your trail winds uphill briefly again and emerges in a "herbaceous opening", a 5-acre clearcut to encourage growth of grass and underbrush for deer browse and small game. Note a bluebird house here. Keep left and aim for a crabapple tree at the head of "Crabtree Lane". After a pleasant glide along this lane, you reach a junction called "Point 6" (a sign says 6), where Crabtree Lane, Old Grade and Broadway trails intersect. *Note: These names have been arbitrarily assigned for purposes of this description. Most trails in gamelands are nameless. We just put tongue in cheek, and call all of these backward trails "S.Seleman" or "Emanon Trail".*

A 2-mile loop starts here at "Point 6". Take Broadway, a broad open swath to your left, gently 1 mile downhill to Range Road. Turn right on the Poleline Path and climb a short hill.

Turn left on a small road and get set for "Orange Juice Hill", a swift ride for skiers. O.J.H. was named when a gentleman skier, after a tumble here, was dismayed to find a yellow liquid running down his leg--until he realized he had sat on the juice in his fanny pack.

Next turn right along Range Road a short way, then right again onto a woods lane. This curves left and then right, up onto the Old Grade, which leads back to Point 6. Then either retrace your way along Crabtree Lane; or continue 0.2 mile east on Old Grade, and turn right at the first cross trail. Emerge in the north side of the "opening". Find the Entrance trail again on the south side of the "opening", and retrace your steps to your car on Sleepy Hollow Drive.

CHAPTER 11
TOW HILL
Three Ponds and a Ghost Town

Summary: <u>3 miles; 2 hours;</u> sandy trails, flat or gentle hills, in the western part of the Barrens/ Gamelands 176. Hike on old roads and rail grade to see remains of an iron-mining town, three very different ponds, and interesting plant life.

Location: 7 miles west of State College. Start from US 322 W.

Features: Development and population pressures are lapping at the edges of this green space. Located in Halfmoon Township, Centre County, PA, this long-forgotten beauty spot has been visited more frequently in recent years, partly due to the proximity of new housing. Since it is part of the Gamelands, hunters will predominate in game seasons, of course. At other times the wide, easy trails are inviting to hikers, x-c skiers and equestrians. Some uncommon plants and abundant birdlife are making it another popular destination for naturalists and conservationists.

History: An iron ore mine was operated by the Juniata Iron and Furnace Company in this area between 1880 and 1895. The town of Tow Hill consisted of about two dozen log houses; a school house for twelve students in grades 1 to 5; two big frame houses for the head boss; a company grocery store and train station; an ore washer, and loading platforms.

Tow Hill may have gotten its name from a type of oil lamp carried by people there, a sort of "Aladdin's lamp", which used tow (flax fibers) as a wick. Some suppose it was named for the tow-colored fields of flax grown there. Another story indicates the name came from "towing" the carts up to the ore pits, and then letting them roll down the hill again.

MAP FOR TOW HILL

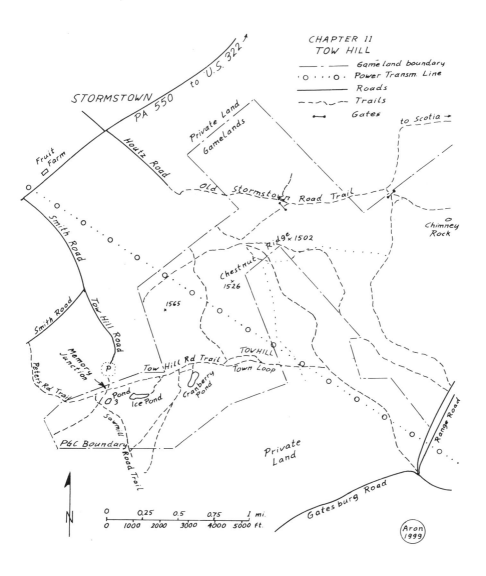

Tow Hill Road was a public road in 1900 until it was vacated in 1928. The US Bureau of Mines assayed the area for iron in 1941, and the small dugout pits which can be seen along the paths may be test pits from this study. In 1942 the area was purchased by the PA Game Commission

Other maps: USGS, Port Matilda and Julian quads; Penn State Outing Club Map 104/105; PA Gazetteer, page 61.

Getting there: Start on US 322 West. About 7 miles northwest of State College, turn left onto PA 550. Follow it about 4 miles, through Stormstown, past Way Fruit Farm, and beyond the big powerline. Turn left on Smith Road. In 1 mile, at the bend, veer left onto Tow Hill Road. Follow it to the circle at the end. Park on the road edge, or a little way down the dirt lane.

Hike description: Begin hiking on the dirt lane heading south. Soon it becomes a trail and enters State Gamelands. Ignore any trails to the left or right. In a few minutes you arrive at a 4-way trail junction. Memorize this spot. Call it *"Memory Junction"*. You will need to recognize it when you return. Got your map and compass? Peters Roadtrail is to the right (west). Sawmill Roadtrail is straight ahead (south). You should turn left (east) to continue on Tow Hill Roadtrail. (*These road names are taken from a plot map provided by local residents Scott and Ginnie Pirmann.*)

It is less than 1 mile to Tow Hill. For now, just follow the mainline path, which is both an old road and an old rail grade. There are some hills, but none of them are very steep. Take note of the side trails you pass. You can visit these on your way back.

In about 1/2 mile the first trail to the right (south) leads to Ice Pond. The intersection looks like two trails, but it is actually a triangle. Soon you will pass near a marsh where an interesting fern grows. Note the chain like pattern of spores on the back.

Next you reach another notable trail junction. To the right, a major unnamed roadtrail heads southwest from here towards Gatesburg. Your main trail, Tow Hill Roadtrail, veers slightly to the left and continues heading east. Some maps show an abandoned sawmill at this junction. A small, shallow pond on the right (south) side of the trail is a good landmark. I call it "*Scum Pond Junction*", but whatever you call it, -- just remember it.

Continuing east on Tow Hill Roadtrail, pass another trail to the right (south) leading to Cranberry Pond. Save it for the return trip.

Pass through a very nice stand of staghorn sumac, so named because of the "velvet" covering on the branches. The red berries are said to make good pink lemonade. Birds enjoy them, too. Their bright red leaves in autumn are eyecatching. No, they are not poisonous; that is a different plant altogether.

Soon you reach the two parallel trails of the town of Tow Hill --the high road and the low road. You can walk the 1/4 mile loop clockwise or reverse. Veer left, uphill to find the high road. Ignore the trail which continues climbing to the left heading back towards Stormstown. Your heading is still east. As you walk along the high road, look to the left and right for ruins of foundations -- houses, ore washer & well-pipes. Continue down the high road until it connects shortly to the right with the parallel low road.

The low road is the actual railroad grade, which continues east and south, and emerges in 2 miles on Gatesburg Road at "The Junction" with Range Road. Don't follow it there today. Instead turn right (west) on the low road and head back along the deep-cut trail. Pretend you are on a train coming into Tow Hill in 1890, and try to imagine what it was like. Look on the hill to your right for remnants of loading docks. Along this low road / rail grade, in May you will find quite a colony of pink lady slippers. Lots of other wildflowers can be found, too, if you are really keen.

On your return trip along Tow Hill Roadtrail you can visit three ponds on side trails to your left (south). The first and largest one is Cranberry Pond, just a short hike down the first sidetrail. It is uncertain if cranberries grow here, but a lot of other things certainly do. This beautiful remote pond, deep in the woods, harbors a variety of wildlife and wildflowers. It makes a nice picnic stop. But please be respectful, quiet and clean in this special place. (*Overnight camping is NOT allowed in state gamelands.*) After your visit, return to the main trail the way you came. Or if you are good at directions, take the shortcut to the left, which goes straight up to "*Scum Pond Junction*".

Still heading west on Tow Hill Roadtrail, the second side trip is to Ice Pond, the middle one of the three ponds. The side trail leading down to it is longer than the one to Cranberry Pond. Along the way you pass a classic beaver dam. Be sure to look around. The beavers have been busy in this area for a long time. Although very different from Cranberry Pond, Ice Pond is also a discovery place. You never know what you will find. It is possible to bushwhack through from here to the next pond, but it is not advisable. The best and easiest is to retrace your way to the main trail; turn left and continue your westward return.

When you get back to "*Memory Junction*", which you memorized at the beginning, you can decide whether to: 1) Turn right and return to your car. or 2) Visit the third pond.

"*Emanon*" Pond is found by heading south on Sawmill Roadtrail, or a short connector. From the 4-way intersection, go west and then south. In a few minutes turn left on a short trail to the pond. It is smaller than the other two ponds, but just as nice. It can be circumnavigated in about 15 minutes, if you are intrepid.

Retrace to "*Memory Junction*" and turn left to reach your car.

CHAPTER 12
TUSSEY RIDGE
Small Walk, Big Views,

Summary: <u>1.5 miles; 1 hour walking time</u>; out and back on a wide, level trail on the ridge in Rothrock State Forest.

Location: 5 miles south of State College. Start on PA 26 S.

Features: On a clear day, or perhaps on a brightly moonlit night, when you want to feel above it all, try this gentle trail. The very young and the very old, and most of those in between, will find this a refreshing leg-stretcher, which can be done after dinner on a summer's eve, or before breakfast on a workday, or during any spare hour. You can walk here through autumn colors or on a snowy day under the unique blueness of a winter sky. This hike may be your introduction to Mid State Trail, an important long-distance foot path in Central PA. You will be meeting the MST often, as it is a part of many of our favorite hikes.

History: The main Mid State Trail begins at U.S. 22 at the junction with Alexandria Road near Water Street in Huntingdon County, and extends to a junction with West Rim Trail north of Blackwell in Tioga County. 276 km (172 miles) of main trail, plus 55 km of major side trails, were completed in 1987. A southern extension, now being built, will add another 126 km, reaching all the way to the Maryland border. The southern part of the Trail is already finished through gamelands #73 to PA 36, and should be finished through Gamelands #97 by mid-1999. A missing link remains, from Everett to PA 36. When completed, the 400 km MST will be the longest trail in Pennsylvania. If you are a serious hiker or backpacker, get yourself a set of maps and guide to the Mid State Trail, available at local outdoor supply stores or from Mid State Trail Association, P.O. Box 167, Boalsburg, PA 16827.

The cost is $15 plus tax and postage ($17.60 total). The price may change with a new edition of the guidebook in 1999. Check first.

Other maps: USGS topo, Pine Grove Mills quad; Purple Lizard Recreation map; Rothrock State Forest map; MSTA map #202.

Getting there: Take PA 26 south (West College Ave.) from State College, about 4 miles to Pine Grove Mills. Turn left at the traffic light, still following PA 26, and drive 2 more miles to the top of Tussey Mountain at the Centre/ Huntingdon County line. Park at the overlook area on the righthand (NW) side of the road.

The overlook has been named " Jo Hays Vista", in honor of a State College man, who served as State Senator from 1955-1962. The view is a pleasing panorama. You can spot the water towers of State College, the domes and cupolas on the Penn State campus, and the farms and forested "barrens" west of State College.

Hike description: Begin your walk at the far end of the parking lot near the county line. Stay on the righthand (N) side of the highway. Pass a gate and follow Mid State Trail, marked with a sign and rectangular orange paint blazes, (SW) along the ridge. Pass a radio tower and reach a clearing with a view to the NW.
The most common tree on this and other ridge tops is the chestnut oak, though this species is almost completely absent in the valleys. Near the clearing, more young maples are beginning to fill the gaps. A summertime wildflower found here is the spotted knapweed.
Continue on the wide, level, orange-blazed trail, passing thicker stands of mountain laurel just before reaching the powerline.

Walk carefully across the rocks to the highest spot, beneath one of the gigantic power towers. The elevation here is 2050 ft. There are views in two directions. To the northwest you can see across farmlands and the low Gatesburg Ridge, with the forested State Gamelands #176 spreading to the west of State College. Beyond, running NE to SW, paralleling Tussey Ridge (the one you're standing on), is Bald Eagle Ridge -- the last ridge of the "ridge and valley" region of Pennsylvania's Appalachians. Beyond Bald Eagle Ridge you can see the broad expanse of the Allegheny Plateau.

To the southeast the view is across the Shaver's Creek and Stone Creek watersheds towards McAlevy's Fort. The wide swath of the powerline can be seen where it crosses Stone Mountain near Greenwood Furnace State Park.

When you have looked your fill, continue a little farther on the trail, entering the woods on the far side of the powerline clearing. A few steps will bring you to a Mid State Trail register inside a country mailbox. Writing your name and comments in this book will help the overseers for this section of trail. It gives them an idea of the number and types of hikers who are using the trail, and any special problems which may arise.

Beyond the trail register the MST continues SW along Tussey Ridge and through the Little Juniata Natural Area to a trailhead on U.S. 22 -- a distance of 32 kilometers (20 miles). This ridgetop trail is difficult to maintain. Bouts with gypsy moths and heavy winter storms bring down many trees, including some with trail blazes. Volunteer overseers do their best to keep the trail open, but more help is always needed. If you would like to help, contact Mid State Trail Association, address listed above. Mid State Trail is still considered one of the wildest, roughest trails in the state. The rocks will chew the boots right off your feet, but spectacular vistas and a sense of isolation make it appealing to many people.

If you are just a short hiker, turn around now and return to your car the way you came. If you would like to do some more ridgetop hiking, consider the Jackson Scenic Trail, which begins from the same overlook parking lot as this one. See the next Chapter.

MAP FOR TUSSEY RIDGE & JACKSON TRAILS

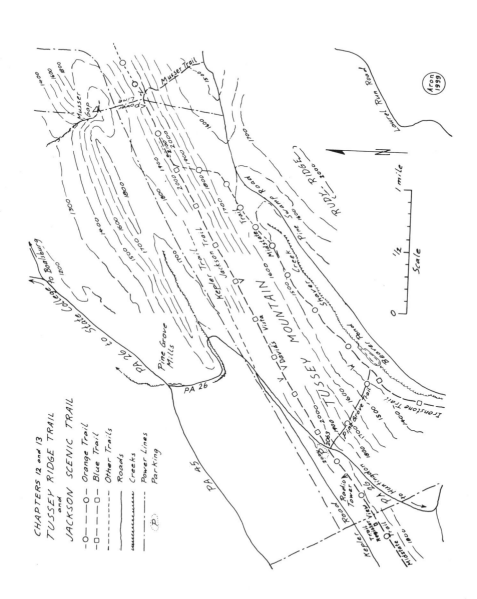

CHAPTER 13
JACKSON SCENIC TRAIL
Longer Walk, Longer Views

See map for Tussey Ridge, page 68.

Summary: 4 miles; 2 to 3 hours walking time; ridgetop trail in Rothrock State Forest; or 6 miles, 3 or 4 hours ridgetop; or a strenuous 6.3 mile loop to the valley and back.

Location: 5 miles south of State College. Start from PA 26 S.

Features: If you like being "high" on a mountain, but can't do the usual requisite climbing to get there, here is a trail for you. Accessible by car in all but the severest winter weather, this one offers an out-and-back walk, somewhat rougher and rockier than the Tussey Ridge hike, but level enough to be called moderate.

History: This trail is named for Evelyn Jackson, a popular and successful student president of the Hiking Division of Penn State Outing Club, sometime in the 1970's. Club activities, including trail clearing, always drew maximum participation under her guidance.

Other maps: USGS topo, Pine Grove Mills & McAlevys Fort quads; Purple Lizard Rec. map; Rothrock State Forest map; MSTA map #202. See also *"Fifty Hikes in Central PA"* by Tom Thwaites.

Getting there: This hike starts from the same parking area as the Tussey Ridge hike (see previous Chapter). Take PA 26 south from State College to Pine Grove Mills. Turn left at the traffic light, still following PA 26 to the top of Tussey Mountain. Park in the Jo Hays Vista parking lot on the righthand side of the road.

Hike description: Look across the highway for a trail sign and BLUE rectangular blazes identifying the Jackson Trail, which heads out along the ridge to the northeast. (The main Mid State Trail, nearby to the right, is orange-blazed and drops down steeply from the south side of the road.) Cross the highway with caution. Begin hiking on the wide jeep trail (gated). After passing a radio equipment building in about half a mile, the trail soon narrows.

David's Vista is the first view to the south. This remote scene above a scree slope overlooking upper Shaver's Creek and the rows of forested ridges beyond, was dedicated in 1998 to the memory of David Kaufman, a gentle hiking man, who admired this view.

On the north side of the ridge after 3/4 mile you pass a USGS triangulation marker and arrive at "Happy Valley Vista", directly above Pine Grove Mills and looking out over farms, villages and metropolitan State College. Continuing along the ridge, there are several more views to the south which overlook densely forested mountainland. Shaver's Creek has its beginnings in the valley directly below. The Mid State Trail passes through there, too. You may catch a glimpse of Pine Swamp Road. The small roundish ridge is Rudy Ridge. Whipple Dam State Park lies hidden beyond.

When you reach the white-blazes which mark a corner of State Forest land, you have walked about 2 miles. Short hikers turn around here and return the way you came for a 4 mile round trip.

Option #2: If you are not yet "half-tired", you can continue for another mile on this trail to the old powerline cut above Musser Gap. The powerlines have been removed, and young saplings are beginning to fill in the old cut. There are still views in both directions. It would then be 3 miles back for a total hike of 6 miles.

Option #3: Turn right on orange-blazed Mid State Trail, and follow it down to Shaver's Creek valley, past Beaver Pond and back up Pine Grove Trail to your car. A 6.3 mile strenuous hike. The steep climb is at the very end of the hike, so it is not recommended for strictly short hikers.

CHAPTER 14
SOUTH IRONSTONE TRAIL
Exercise and Learning

Summary: <u>4.5 miles; 3 hours walking time;</u> steep downhill, then along a stream. The land is within Rothrock State Forest and PSU Experimental Forest. This is a shuttle hike. Take two cars.

Location: 7 miles south of State College. Start from PA 26 S.

Features: South Ironstone is part of a 10.6 mile blue-blazed trail, which runs from the Mid State Trail at the top of Indian Steps Trail, past Stone Valley Recreation Area (see following two chapters), and back again to Mid State Trail at Beaver Pond. The entire Ironstone Loop, including a piece of Mid State Trail on Tussey Ridge, is 14.3 miles. It is a good long dayhike, or a modest backpack, but is too long and rugged for short hikers. However, the south section is mellow enough, passing over varied terrain near water. The kids should enjoy getting their feet muddy. In any case, it is a nice change from hiking on rocky ridges.

Other maps: Rothrock State Forest map; MSTA map #202; USGS topo, Pine Grove Mills quad; Purple Lizard Rec. map.

Getting there: From State College take PA 26 south. Turn left in Pine Grove Mills and cross Tussey Mountain. 2 miles beyond the overlook turn right at the Monroe Furnace intersection onto the Petersburg Road. Signs point to Stone Valley Recreation Area. At the signs for East Entrance, turn left into the Stone Valley Recreation Area. Take the right fork of the entrance road to Shaver's Creek Environmental Center and leave car #2 in the parking lot. This is the end point of the hike. Now take car #1 and return the way you came to the PA 26 overlook above Pine Grove Mills (Jo Hays Vista). Take some time to admire the view.

MAP FOR IRONSTONE TRAIL

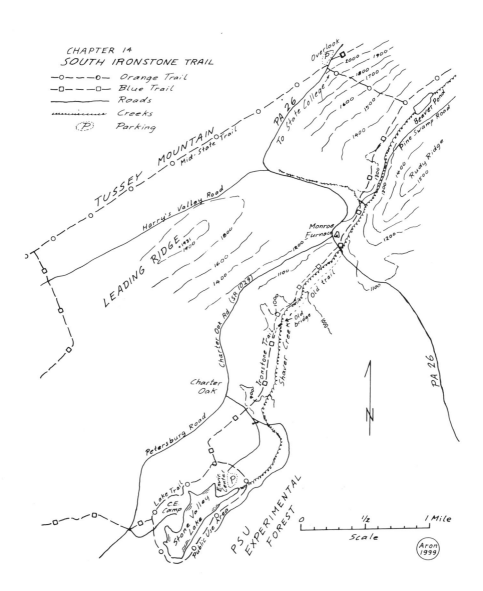

CHAPTER 14
SOUTH IRONSTONE TRAIL

—o— — —o— Orange Trail
—□— — —□— Blue Trail
——————— Roads
············· Creeks
(P) Parking

Note: for an even shorter hike, a car could be stationed at the Monroe Furnace intersection -- the halfway point of your hike.

Hike description: Your hike starts on Pine Grove Trail/ MST, across the road from the PA 26 overlook. It is blazed with orange rectangles and descends quite steeply for about 3/4 of a mile.

Downhill can be almost as difficult as uphill. A walking stick may be helpful, whether it is an Alpine souvenir, an Irish shillelagh, or just a stout stick which helps to balance and support you.

There are a few tulip trees along this section. One seldom sees the blossoms because the leaves emerge first and tend to hide the flowers on these tall trees. After the bloom in June, you may find some orange and cream petals dropped on the ground.

At the bottom of the hill you reach a signed junction. Before pursuing the Ironstone Trail, you should make an interesting side trip to Beaver Pond. Turn and walk to the left (on MST orange) for just 100 yards or so, and then find your way down to the Pond. This area used to belong to Penn State University, but is once again a part of Rothrock State Forest. A waterfowl habitat project was started but then scrapped, apparently because it conflicted with the needs of a scarce species of dragonfly.

The earthen dam was NOT built by beavers. (Neither was Beaver Stadium.) The pond is slowly filling in and becoming a meadow, but a few frogs and salamanders, dragon flies, and bog plants can be found. Shaver's Creek begins here.

Now find your way back to the signed junction and continue your hike. Follow the blue-blazed Ironstone Trail downstream on old charcoal roads and new trail, crossing one small stream, and Pine Swamp Road. Just before the trail reaches PA 26 again, you'll see the ruins of Monroe Furnace, a reminder of a chapter in PA history which left many of these old iron furnaces, like pyramids, dotting the landscape. Your hike is about half over. Take a short break.

Cross PA 26 cautiously, and climb over the steel guardrail. The blue-blazed trail crosses the open powerline right-of-way, and re-enters the cool hemlock woods, still following along the right bank (north side) of Shaver's Creek. This part of the trail used to follow a dirt road on the south side of the stream. It was relocated to the north side because the dirt track was being churned up by 4WD vehicles. This side of the stream is much prettier than the former route, but some of it is rougher going, and you may get your feet wet. Soon the trail rejoins its former route at Woodcock Trail. Backtrack on the old route a few steps to reach a neat little footbridge, a good lunch stop. Check quietly for shy brook trout.

The trail continues along Woodcock Trail, one of the instructional areas of Shaver's Creek Environmental Center. After you cross the East Entrance Road, it is about 3/4 mile to the Center. Follow the blazed trail through a spruce and red pine plantation, across a small hill and then turn left and follow a little valley beside a rivulet. In April you may see rue anemone blooming, and later, mayapples and golden ragwort and wild ginger. We spotted a woodcock there.

In about half a mile the trail is joined by an orange-blazed Lake Trail. (See next chapter.) Bear left onto a wide trail which curves up past the sugar shack (maple syrup boiling shed) to the Environmental Center on the hilltop. Be sure to visit the Center sometime. Their displays are interesting to all ages with plenty to see and touch, even live frogs, snakes and turtles. Visit the Raptor Center out back to see the bald eagles and various hawks and owls. Field guides and nature books are sold in the bookstore.

Short memory? Remember to pick up car #1 at the overlook on your way home.

CHAPTER 15
STONE VALLEY
Nature Surrounding

Summary: 3 miles; 2 hours walking time; around the lake. The facilities at Stone Valley Recreation Area are administered by Penn State University. The trail system has been upgraded and extended. Trails are blazed in many colors. An improved map of hiking and x-c skiing trails is available at the Environmental Center for $2.50.

Location: 9 miles south of State College. Start from PA 26 S.

Features: This area cannot be fully described in a simple chapter, nor fully seen and appreciated in just one trip. During repeated visits in all seasons of the year, one may begin to get a feeling for the varied habitats and natural cycles of plants and animals which are abundantly present around 72-acre Lake Perez. The Recreation area and Shaver's Creek Environmental Center are crown jewels of the University. If you are learning to love nature, plan to come here often. Besides an extensive hiking trail system, the lake also offers fishing, canoeing, sailing, and in winter, ice skating and cross-country skiing -- a true Mecca for those seeking sun and fresh air, exercise or relaxation. Rental equipment is available.

The Center itself has much to offer--a raptor aviary for injured birds of prey, herb gardens; varied new programs; and a maple sugar shack. Stone Valley and Shaver's Creek must be explored over and over again. Go see for yourself.

Other maps: USGS topo, Pine Grove Mills quad; Rothrock State Forest map; MSTA map #202; Purple Lizard Rec. map; Stone Valley Recreation Area Trails Map. Also *More Outbound Journeys in Pennsylvania* by Marcia Bonta.

Getting there: From State College take PA 26 south. Turn left in Pine Grove Mills and cross Tussey Mountain. 2 miles beyond the Jo Hays Vista turn right onto the paved SR 1029, called Charter Oak or Petersburg Road. Follow signs to Stone Valley Recreation Area. Turn left into the East Entrance road. Take the right fork of the entrance road to Shaver's Creek Environmental Center and park in the lot. Take the short path to the Center. Your hike begins and ends here.

Inside the Center you will find maps for sale, a nature museum, a bookstore, and friendly helpful people. Just ask. Restrooms are in another building down the path beyond the raptor cages.

Hike description: Begin your hike on the orange-blazed Lake Trail which descends from the bus parking lot near a large sugar maple tree. The first flower of spring, seen here in March or April, is the coltsfoot (often mistaken for a dandelion). It was brought to this country by early settlers, who used it in a honeyed brew as a cough medicine.

Continue down through a tamarack (larch) plantation. These trees are the exception to the rule. They are needle trees which are not evergreen. They lose their needles every fall like broad-leaved deciduous trees.

Near the first trail intersection, where a red-blazed path leads to a boardwalk across the marsh, (currently closed for repairs) you'll find all 3 of the most common vines in the woods-- Virginia creeper, wild grapevine, and poison ivy. Learn to distinguish them.

Follow the orange path. Notice yellow violets and sweet white violets and even violet violets, and also jack-in-the-pulpits growing in the moist woods.

MAP FOR STONE VALLEY TRAILS

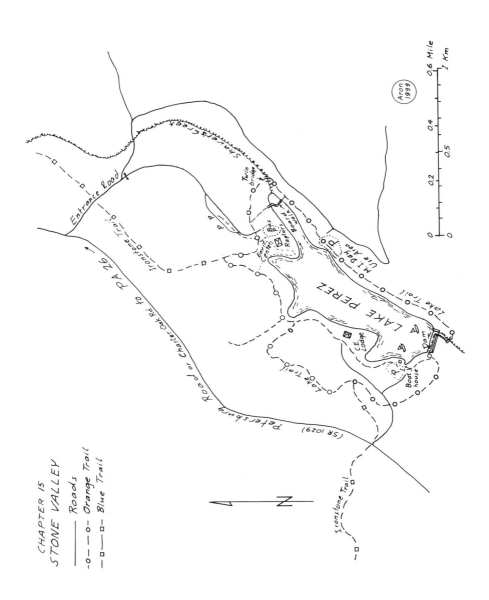

Continue on the orange-blazed Lake Trail passing an entrance to the white-blazed Black Walnut Trail. Cross Shaver's Creek on twin bridges. The two bridges are now linked in the middle, because the island which used to separate them was mostly under water. The beavers have been busy indeed. A sizable beaverdam in the early 1990s nearly inundated the whole trail. Beavers are the only mammals, other than humans, who significantly change their environment. Their diet consists of tree bark, twigs and leaves, so they are constantly gnawing on trees to keep their stomachs filled, and also to keep their ever-growing incisors worn down. Evidence of beavers' dining and dentistry is readily found around here.

After the bridges, turn right on the orange path. Look for skunk cabbage in the marshy edges. Make a side trip to the boardwalk (if repairs are finished.) Walk out quietly and look and listen for birds feeding or nesting around the shallow end of the lake. On the boardwalk you can keep your feet dry while peering into the water for critters and plants--frogs, salamanders; cattails, skunk cabbage, swamp alders; red-winged blackbirds and tree swallows.

Return to the orange trail and continue your clockwise progress around the lake. In spring look for bloodroot, wild ginger, Indian cucumber root, fringed polygala, bishop's cap, wild geranium, hepatica, marsh marigold, dwarf ginseng, buttercup -- to name a few. Here is a paradise of ephemeral wildflowers.

The trail crosses the parking lot of the MI (Mineral Industries) Day Use Area, passes the canoe rental docks near the picnic area, shaded by tall pines. In winter cross-country skis or ice skates can be rented here. During spring and fall migrations, check the lake for water birds--loons, gulls, mergansers, grebes, or a great blue heron.

Next the trail goes down to the left of the spillway and crosses a footbridge below the dam. It then comes back up along the other side of the spillway to a wooden stairway on the dam. An old footway which used to cut diagonally across the face of the dam should no longer be used, because of erosion problems. Walk across the dam top and enjoy the views across the lake and up to Tussey Ridge.

On the other side of the dam the trail forks. Both the orange-blazed Lake Trail on the left and the unblazed lakeside trail on the right will take you around the lake. If you are on x-c skis, or are insecure on a narrow trail, you'll want to stay on the orange. But the orange is farther from the water, and a little bit longer. Since there are some interesting things to see on the lakeside trail, let's choose it today. (Watch your step; it may be steep and muddy.) Follow it around past the sailboat docks. You may see a butterfly-- a somber mourning cloak or a cheerful tiger swallowtail.

Pass around the upper end of the marsh. Plants in or near the marsh include black-eyed Susan, goldenrod, gill-over-the-ground, cattails; and on the drier hillside--yellow cinquefoil, violets, pussytoes, and speedwell. A brown thrasher was heard singing in this area in late April. He is one of the mimic birds who copy songs from other species. The varied song of the brown thrasher is identifiable because he sings everything twice -- unlike the mockingbird, who repeats a phrase many times -- or the catbird, who usually does not repeat phrases, but presents the listener with an incredible virtuoso concert before giving himself away with a meowing call.

Also seen in this area in May were kingbirds, handsome aerial acrobats who have an unusual taste for bees; and orioles, not the baseball team, but the orange and black, opera-voiced birds who love to eat caterpillars.

Go past the CE (Civil Engineering) Lodge and Outdoor School camp area, keeping the lake on your right. The trail is quite high above the water here. If you're lucky, in late summer you may see closed gentian blooming.

Soon the trail rejoins the orange Lake Trail. (The blue blazes of Ironstone Trail coincide with the orange for about a mile.) Continue with the lake on your right. Cross a wooden footbridge, and go through a red pine forest; you might see or hear a pileated woodpecker, or the square holes this big bird has made in trees.

When you reach the junction where Ironstone Trail turns off towards Beaver Pond, turn right and follow the orange up the wide jeep trail, which curves up the hill to the Environmental Center. A small sugar shack, where they boil maple syrup in February, is just to the right. Look for pink lady slippers in late May.

You should plan on returning often to the Stone Valley Lake area. Other trails for you to explore include the white-blazed Black Walnut Trail, the blue-blazed north section of the Ironstone Trail, the Homestead Trail and many others. In winter, cross-country ski trails are popular. Don't walk in the ski tracks if you can avoid it, as this ruins them for skiers. But you can follow these paths when the snow is gone. The number for the Recreation Area is 814-863-0762. Call to find out about trail conditions.

For more information about what is happening in and around the Environmental Center, call 814-863-2000. Many well-led activities are available for a small fee. You can become a member, and/ or volunteer. Help is always needed. Working or playing, it can be a highly enjoyable place to spend the day.

CHAPTER 16
INDIAN STEPS
Sure You Can

Summary: 4 miles; 3 hours walking time; a steep climb, some stone steps, a rocky ridge with vistas, and an easy return.

Location: 8 miles SW of State College. Start from PA 26 S.

Features & History: For many years the Indian Steps trail has been a popular hike for scout troops and school groups. The trail climbs Tussey Mountain and joins the Mid State Trail on the ridge It has a reputation of being one of the steepest trails around here. It does indeed go straight up the side of one of our larger mountains at one of the steepest points. There are actual "steps" near the top of the trail -- large rocks, rearranged to make walking more convenient. Other than that, this inconveniently located path connects "nowhere" to "nothing", and is probably not of Indian origin. More likely, it began as a log skid. It is a good exercise hike, and not as difficult as you think. The rise is only 500 ft. over 1/3 mile. Westerners would scoff to hear us call it a mountain.

Other maps: USGS topo, Pine Grove Mills quad; Rothrock State Forest map; MSTA map #202; Purple Lizard Rec. map. Also see *50 Hikes in Central PA, by Tom Thwaites.*

Getting there: Take PA 26 south to Pine Grove Mills. Turn left at the traffic light, and follow PA 26, over the mountain. About 1 mile down the south side, turn right onto a gravel forestry road -- Harry's Valley Road. Check your odometer at the turnoff, because the trail is easily missed. Drive exactly 2 miles. Look for a blue-blazed trail, with a sign (Crownover Trail), on the right (north) side. Drive a short distance beyond the trail. There is a turnoff on the left where you can turn the car around. Park on the roadside.

Hike description: Walk back on the road to the blue trail and begin your climb. Pace yourself. Breathe regularly and deeply. Take short steps. Stop a few times and check the view. It gets better as you go up. (the higher up, the mucher.) Tell the kids to wait for you at the top. There is a circle of stones on the top where many groups have gathered to await the slower members of their party. (The faster ones get to rest longer.)

When you have rested, regrouped, and refreshed yourselves with your canteen of water -- you didn't forget, did you! -- proceed, turning left (southwest) on the orange-blazed Mid State Trail. This is typical ridge top -- chestnut oak, mountain laurel, huckleberries (yummy in summer) and plenty of rocks. Watch for a sign--"view" to the right (north) in 1/4 mile. From this spot above PA 45 near Rocksprings, site of Penn State's Ag Progress Days in August, you can look across Nittany Valley towards Fairbrook and the Barrens. Later you pass an area with more hemlock trees near the north side. You may notice deer sign on the trail or even be privileged to see a deer or two bounding away with flashing white tails.

In a mile there is a sign -- H2O -- indicating that water is available down a side trail on the north slope. The guidebook reveals that this spring is 73 meters down the trail. If you really need water, send a nimble person to fill the canteens. Otherwise just continue on the orange trail.

Not far beyond the H2O sign the trail comes out onto some large rocks with an open view to the south. You can break out your lunch here and sit and admire the world. Stone Valley's Lake Perez is visible a little to the left in your view. It looks like two small lakes because a hill cuts the view in two. You can see the pine forest behind the M.I. Day Use Area and make out the dam on the righthand side of the lake from here.(Or not, depending on the clarity of day and your eyesight.)

MAP FOR INDIAN STEPS

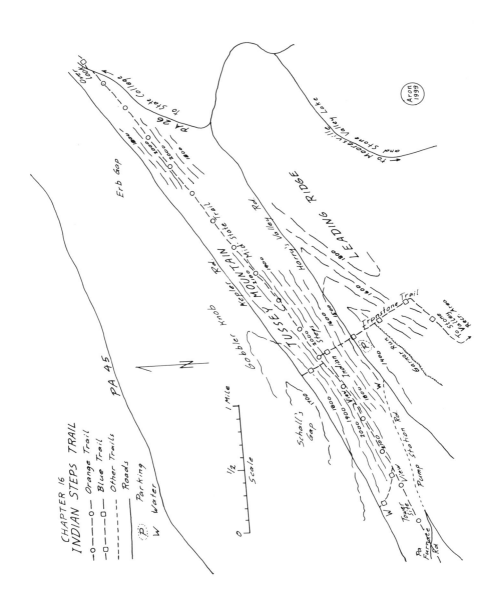

In another half mile you come to the site of the former Tussey Mountain Fire Tower. It was dismantled in 1978 after the state failed to lease it to any group interested in preserving it. Although 10 or 12 groups expressed interest, it was learned that state rules would prohibit anyone from using the tower or even camping at its base and that the lessee would have considerable maintenance expense and would have to erect an 8-foot cyclone fence around it. Thus all interest disappeared and so did the firetower.

Continue past the tower site to the gate at Pennsylvania Furnace Road. Leaving the orange Mid State Trail now, turn left (south) on the road and follow it down, basking in views as you descend. The road soon makes an acute switchback to the right, but you continue straight ahead on an old road trail (Pump Station Road) which is wide and grassy and brings you down the mountain at an angle on an easy slope, with a couple more views. There is some witch hazel growing about halfway down. In October you may see its wispy greenish yellow blossoms. This contrary shrub blooms in the fall of the year rather than spring.

After a mile on Pump Station Road trail you come out on Harry's Valley Road. Turn left and follow it half a mile to your car.

Bonus hike: North Ironstone Trail. Starting from the same place where the Indian Steps hike starts, the blue-blazed Ironstone Trail (Crownover Tr.), crosses Harry's Valley Road going south, and descends to Garner Run. It then climbs Leading Ridge on stone steps, turns right along the ridge, then follows a dirt road down and varied paths through the woods into the Stone Valley Recreation Area. It is the northern part of Ironstone Loop (see South Ironstone chapter). It is a bit rougher, and longer than the other short hikes -- more than 6 miles, but it is an interesting hike which you may want to try sometime. Just follow the blue blazes.

CHAPTER 17
WHIPPLE DAM
A Small Green Circle

Summary: <u>2 to 3 miles; 1 to 2 hours</u>. Make a circle around this State Park and lake on easy woods roads or trails. Bring the whole family. Young and old can enjoy this very manageable outing.

Location: 7 miles south of State College. Start from PA 26 S.

Features: This small park contains only 256 acres, and the lake is just 22 acres. Yet it has as much to offer as many of the larger parks. Enjoy fishing around the dam in spring, swimming at the beach in summer, ice skating and x-c skiing in winter. Picnics and hiking are fun any time. In the designated Laurel Run Natural Area in and around the park, you may find beaver dams and lodges; pink lady slippers, azalea; chickadees, ducks, or even a bald eagle. Park management plans call for a scenic wetlands overlook and lakeside trail, and an exhibit kiosk to display information about historic activities like iron mining, the Whipple sawmill, and the CCC.

History: The Whipple family operated a sawmill at the original dam, downstream from here. In 1928 the Commonwealth of Pennsylvania built a new dam at a better location upstream. In 1936 the Civilian Conservation Corps built the present dam and recreation facilities around the lake. Designated in 1937 as a National Historic District, Whipple Dam was a work site of one of the Depression-Era's most important relief programs, the CCC.

Other maps: PA Highway Map; PA Gazetteer, page 62; Rothrock State Forest map; Purple Lizard Recreational map; USGS topo/ McAlevys Fort quad; Whipple Dam State Park map.

Getting there: Follow PA 26 (West College Ave.) south to Pine Grove Mills. Turn left and drive over Tussey Mountain. Stay on

page 85

PA 26 for about 10 miles. Turn left at the sign for Whipple Dam State Park, and follow the signs 1/2 mile to the park entrance. Parking, shelters, public phone, comfort stations, and other amenities are found near the beach on the south side of the lake.

Hike description: You could lose yourself in the laurel, exploring the wet woods at the upper end of the lake, looking for beaver sign, and other interesting discoveries.

If you just want to hike around the lake with dry feet, begin walking east on the park road along the lake. Follow the one way road to where it joins Laurel Run Road. Keep left and continue along the forestry road. Look for flowers; Listen for birds. In about 1/2 mile, watch for a hunting cabin, visible on a small road to the left. Turn sharp left (west) onto a narrow dirt road. This is Beidler Road. Pass the cabin. Cross Laurel Run on the old road bridge. Look for fish in the stream.

Continue along Beidler Road, going uphill, heading southwest. At the top in 1/4 mile, turn left to find the parallel Ridge Trail running to your left through a forest of young pine. From the ridge you may catch some glimpses of the natural area of Laurel Run, and the park and lake below. The Ridge Trail, merges with Beidler Rd. again in 1/2 mile at a trail junction. Look for pink lady slippers.

If you are in a hurry to get back, you can short cut down the steeper Table Top Trail, which turns left (south) down to the park. But to avoid the steep downhill, stay on the Road/Trail and let it bring you gently down the last half mile to join the park exit road, Whipple Road.

Follow Whipple Road left (east) towards the lake. Explore the north lakeside if you have time. Look for bright pink azalea. Walk to the lookout. Then walk back towards the dam. Look for ferns on the rock cliff near the dam as you head for your car.

MAP FOR WHIPPLE DAM

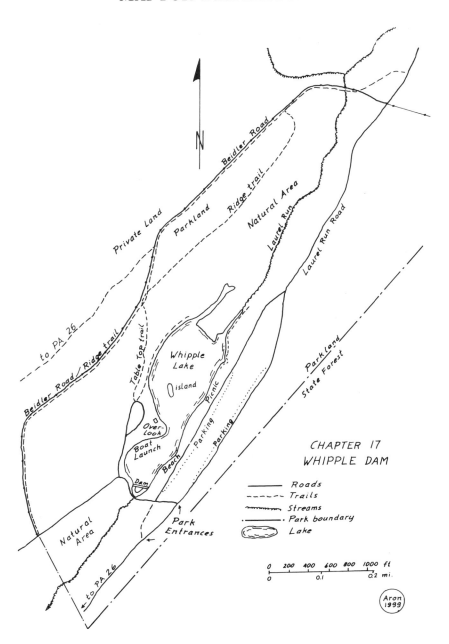

N

Beidler Road

Private Land

Parkland

Ridge trail

Natural Area

Laurel Run

Laurel Run Road

to PA 26

Beidler Road / Ridge trail

Table Top trail

Whipple Lake

island

Picnic

Parkland State Forest

Over-look

Boat Launch

Parking

Parking

Beach

Dam

Natural Area

Park Entrances

to PA 26

CHAPTER 17
WHIPPLE DAM

——————	Roads
- - - - - -	Trails
∼∼∼∼∼	Streams
- • - • -	Park boundary
⬭	Lake

0   200 400 600 800 1000 ft

0   0.1   0.2 mi.

Aron
1999

CHAPTER 18
LITTLE FLAT
The Sky Is the Limit

Summary: <u>6 miles; 4 hours walking time</u>. Climb Tussey Mountain to its highest point at the firetower, using newly reopened trails. Return by descending the short steep Kettle Trail, and hiking back 2 miles on the easier Lonberger x-c ski Path. This is a good sampling of trails, old and new in Rothrock State Forest land.

Location: 6 miles ESE of State College. Start from US 322 E.

Features: Little Flat Firetower, at 2400+ ft. elevation, is the highest point on the Mid State Trail and probably the highest you will ever get on a mountain in Centre County. Up here, thoughts can go soaring. You are on a kind of small scale "continental divide". Streams arising within a few miles from here flow in all directions. Some rush north to Bald Eagle Creek, some go east into Penn's Creek, and others prefer to head south and west to Stone Creek and the Little Juniata. Although all of these waters eventually end up in the Susquehanna, it is interesting to contemplate how many different ways there are to the same end. Now think of all the implications and applications of that statement, and let your own thoughts soar.

This loop offers gradual climbs and steep descents: plus vistas, blueberries, and variable scenery on moderate trails, featuring typical mountaintop flora and fauna.

History: The hike starts from a new State Forest parking lot in Galbraith Gap, provided by DCNR, Rothrock Forest District. This area in the Gap, a 20.7-acre tract, was formerly part of the Harris Township Water System, which was sold to State College Water Authority in 1995. After studying this corner of rocky bluffs, and hemlock shaded mountain stream, a committee of township residents and other persons, from planning agencies, conservancies, adjacent property owners, water authorities and the Bureau of Forestry reached (astoundingly) unanimous agreement that "the highest and best use" for those acres would be as recreational lands. Subsequently in 1996 it was transferred for a nominal sum to DCNR/ Rothrock State Forest District. Plans call for enhancements such as the parking lot, and informational signs and kiosks or educational bulletin boards.

Other maps: USGS topo, State College, McAlevy's Fort, Centre Hall, & Barrville quads; Rothrock State Forest map; MSTA map #203; Purple Lizard Recreation map. Also see *50 Hikes in Central PA* by Tom Thwaites.

Getting there: From US 322 two miles east of Boalsburg, turn right to Tussey Mountain Ski Area and follow Bear Meadows Road about 1 mile. At the sign for Rothrock State Forest Parking Lot, turn left into the short entrance drive up to the gravel parking lot.

Hike description: To minimize road walking, begin your hike on the old grade trail which is above the Galbraith Gap lot where you parked. This old road runs above the remnants of the old reservoir and emerges soon on Bear Meadows Road. Turn right for a short distance, cross the road bridge and then turn left again, ducking back into the woods on a blue-blazed trail on an old rail grade which follows the south bank of Galbraith Gap Run for 1/4 mile. It comes out on Laurel Run Road near the forestry gate.

Just across the road, look for a sign and a trail going uphill, parallel with, and to the left of, a small run coming from Spruce Gap. This new trail is just outside State Forest land. Be respectful of property rights. (Hikers used to use a nearby driveway which goes up to a private camp, but the new trail eliminates the need to use the private drive, or cross the stream, and skips part of a steep climb on a very steep S-curve trail.) Follow the newer path up to a signed trail intersection with Spruce Gap Trail and Lonberger Path, (named for Fred Lonberger, a state forester from Boalsburg, who worked in this area for several decades, in the 1940's and again after WWII. He also operated the sawmill at Whipple Dam.) This trail junction is about a half mile from your car. You will use the same trail sequence on your return.

Continue your upward quest by following Spruce Gap Trail initially, until a section of Lonberger Path known as Three Bridges veers off to the right, around the hollow on an even grade, crossing streamlets on three wooden bridges. Officially "Spruce Gap", the hollow is more colorfully known by locals as "Hoofty Hollow". After passing the spring and a short piece of trail, you emerge at the bend on Laurel Run Road again, having shortcut a mile of it. Find a post sign here. *The official Lonberger Path x-c ski trail follows Laurel Run Road to this point, rather than climbing the steep sections you have just done, and avoiding private land.*

Heading up Laurel Run Road, look to the left for the blue-blazed trail called "Old Laurel Run Road". The original road was here. The old route was deeply imbedded in the mountain side, but nearly lost -- buried beneath accumulated blowdowns and invading mountain laurel bushes. About 1996 or 1997 this trail and others in the Galbraith Gap area were reopened. Working with the Bureau of Forestry and a few others, a determined trail builder named Tom Smyth put a big chunk of his spare time into building trails in the newly acquired Galbraith Gap area. His touch is also found in Shingletown Gap and on Mount Nittany. Such dedicated volunteers are a rare species, but they form the backbone of trail maintenance in Pennsylvania.

The climb on Old Laurel Run Road is very gradual. The total vertical rise is 600 ft. in 1 mile. The trail joins Little Flat Tower Road, which at this point is also orange-blazed Mid State Trail. Turn left and follow the road to Little Flat Tower.

MAP FOR LITTLE FLAT

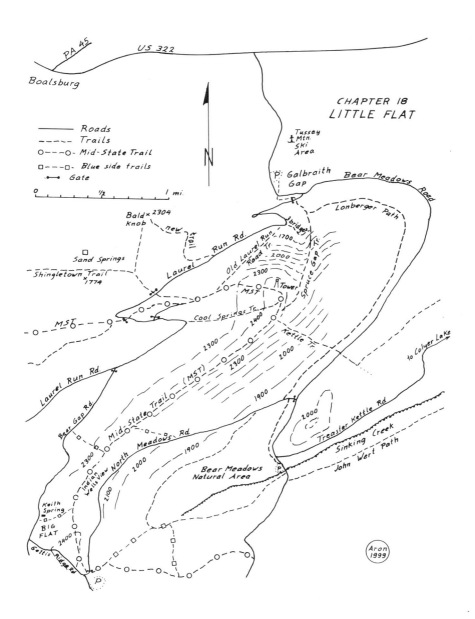

Boalsburg

PA 45 US 322

CHAPTER 18
LITTLE FLAT

Tussey
Mtn.
Ski
Area

P. Galbraith
Gap

Bear Meadows Road

Lonberger Path

Roads
Trails
Mid-State Trail
Blue side trails
Gate

0   ½   1 mi.

Bald × 2304
Knob

new trail

Laurel Run Rd.

Old Laurel Run Road

1700

bridge

2000

Spruce Gap Tr.

Sand Springs

Shingletown Trail
1774

2300

R Tower

MST

Cool Springs Tr.

MST

2400

Kettle Tr.

2300

2300

2000

1900

to Colyer Lake

Mid-State Trail (MST)

Laurel Run Rd.

Bear Gap Rd.

2300

Indian Wells View North Meadows Rd.

2000

1900

2000

1000

Treaster Kettle Rd.

Sinking Creek

John Wert Path

Bear Meadows
Natural Area

Keith
Spring

BIG
FLAT

2400

Geltis Ridge Rd.

P

Aron
1999

The tower itself is still used by the Bureau of Forestry and is manned during periods of high fire danger. Many acres around the tower are covered only by small shrubs, mainly lowbush blueberries (huckleberries). Earlier, when the tower was accessible by car in the summertime, many people used to come here in July and August to gather berries. Visiting bears and an occasional rattlesnake might also be found here. Please walk carefully so as not to frighten these extremely shy creatures.

Because of repeated vandalism, the Bureau of Forestry was forced to keep the gate to Little Flat Tower Road locked. Damage to signs, gates and locks, windows, and to the firetower and its equipment have been costly. Good citizens, please be on the lookout and promptly report any observed damage or misconduct. The number for Rothrock District Forest office in Huntingdon is (814) 643-2340. For local police, fire, or ambulance dial 911.

The lookout tower can be climbed at your own risk. There are spectacular views on a clear day, although the trees nearby are getting a bit too tall now. You can look north over Mt. Nittany, northeast to the oval knob called "Egg Hill" which thrusts itself up in the middle of Penn's Valley. To the south you may be able to spot the other lookout tower -- Greenwood Tower on Broad Mountain in Huntingdon County, about 5.25 air miles away.

History II: Little Flat Tower is the halfway and highpoint of your hike. Perhaps this is the appropriate place to add a word about the Mid State Trail, and the man who made it happen.

The Mid State Trail is one you will encounter repeatedly in this book. This long-distance trail is the basis and lifeline of many hikes in Central PA. It had its beginnings at Little Flat where the first piece of trail was cleared by Penn State Outing Club in September, 1969. By 1987 the main trail -- 276 kilometers -- , plus 55 km of side trail, was complete. When the southern extension is completed, MST will be over 400 km -- the longest trail in Pennsylvania.

The Mid State Trail likes to follow the ridge tops. Many hikers complain about the rocks and brush and lack of springs, so why build a trail up there? For one thing ridge tops are more often public land and contain noncommercial forest. In short, nobody else wanted it. Besides, it offers spectacular views, which tend to inspire people. Here is an example:

> *"We came to the edge of the ridge, rounded a turn, and there it was, illuminated by the setting sun, and yet crystal clear. Below us a wood thrush sang and we could hear the waters of Slate Run rushing towards Pine Creek and the Chesapeake."*

That particular vista was on the Black Forest Trail. It was 1972, and the inspired person, quoted here from a 1985 article on the history of Mid State Trail, was Thomas T. Thwaites. He goes on to comment about a firetower visible in the view:

> *"The firetower bespoke of stewardship rather than dominion over this rugged, beautiful but peaceful landscape. It was as if the secrets of the universe were laid bare before you, if you could only recognize them."*

Tom Thwaites, as hiking advisor to the Penn State Outing Club, was already involved in trail building then, having led the club on its first effort at Little Flat in 1969, but inspirational vistas like that one have kept him going. He became a "vista man", whose belief that *"a satisfying trail is not the shortest route but the most interesting route"*, steered the Mid State Trail onto the ridges, past firetowers, and through state parks, forests and green circles across the state.

Tom Thwaites was the inveterate trail builder who was the driving force behind the creation of Mid State Trail, and who continues to forge ahead, extending the trail south to the Maryland border. Founding the Mid State Trail Association in 1982, and serving as its president, he is making sure the trail is maintained, signed, and provided with maps and guidebook. A Penn State associate professor in physics, now retired, Thwaites continues to co-ordinate KTA's TrailCare Team working on many PA trails. He is the author of all three books, in the *"Fifty Hikes"* series in Pennsylvania -- *Central, Western, and Eastern PA.* He has received many honors for his work on trails. Keystone Trails Association presented him with their Citation Award "for distinguished service to the cause of hiking" in 1985. In 1988 he received a "Take Pride in Pennsylvania" award from the governor; followed in July 1989 by a visit to the White House in Washington, D.C. to receive a "Take Pride in America" award, for his work in conserving our natural heritage and involving many others in the process. If there is one man who stands above all the rest for having positively affected HIKING in Pennsylvania, it is Thomas T. Thwaites. All hikers' hats are off in tribute to him.

After you have received your inspiration from the tower, there are **several options for a return trip.**

1)Return the way you came, for a round trip of 5 miles.

2)The shortest way: Follow MST into the woods a short way. Turn left on Spruce Gap Trail; descend 1 mile down a steep, loose trail -- not recommended for neophytes. Total round trip 3.5 miles.

3)The roadwalk: Turn right off MST on Cool Spring Trail (sometimes called Laurel Run Trail), descend 1 fairly steep mile to a wide curve of Laurel Run Road near Fleet Foot hunting camp. The "Cool Spring" mentioned on the trail sign is at the camp. Turn right and walk uphill on the road. After 0.3 mile you pass the gated entrance to Little Flat Tower Road. Continue another 0.2 mile to the summit, where Mid State Trail crosses Laurel Run Road. You may remember this spot as the trailhead for Skyline Trail. Following the road about 4 miles back to your car makes a total hike of 6.5 miles.(2.5 up and 4 down) A variation would be to follow the Tower Road and Laurel Run Road. This all-road, all-downhill way would be the preferred route back on x-c skis.

4)The most varied and interesting return route uses Kettle Trail and Lonberger Path as follows: From the Tower, turn right on MST and follow it about 1/4 mile. Turn left at the signed Kettle Trail. This unblazed trail descends quite steeply at first, heading straight down the mountainside. Take great care crossing the rock piles at the top. The going is difficult for the first few minutes, but gradually improves as the grade lessens, and the rocks thin out. The last part, cut through mountain laurel, is good footway.

When you reach a signed junction with Lonberger Path, turn left. Follow the blue-blazed x-c ski trail 2 miles, curving around the base of the mountain to the trail junction with Spruce Gap Trail. Remember this spot? Retrace your steps down the 1/2 mile of trails back to your car at the Galbraith Gap parking lot.

Bonus hike: One Way Downhill. Here is a good fall hike. Set up a shuttle. Leave one car at Galbraith Gap. Drive out Bear Meadows Road 3+ miles. Turn right on North Meadows Road and drive 2+ miles to the top. Park at the intersection with Gettis Ridge Road. The hike back from here takes you past many vistas on Big Flat and Little Flat along 3.5 miles of Mid State Trail; then from Little Flat Tower you can descend gently via Tower Road, Old Laurel Run Road Trail, Three Bridges, Lonberger, etc. for a total hike of 5.5 miles.

CHAPTER 19
BIG FLAT
A Mountain Too Big to Hug

Summary: 3.2 miles; 2 hours walking time. Mostly level walking on a wide mountain; a view; a cool drink; mountain laurel blooming in June, fall color in October, cross-country skiing in February; a wildlife retreat year around.

Location: 6 miles SSE of State College. Start from US 322 E.

Features: Big Flat can seem like the top of the world. Splendidly isolated, it is as much a feeling as a place, a sort of fourth dimension. Whether drinking-in the view from Indian Wells or cool water from Keith Spring, I LOVE THIS MOUNTAIN. You are likely to find tracks of deer, bear and others in the mud or snow. The whole ridge stands tall at 2300 to 2400 feet. Snow lies deep here long after it is gone from the valley, making the area almost inaccessible in winter, except on skis. This adds to the isolation and charm. Big Flat is the broad, other end of the ridge where Little Flat sits. The ridge and the piece of Mid State Trail connecting the two "flats" is only 3.25 miles long. And Big Flat, the part above 2300 ft., is half a mile wide. Located in Rothrock State Forest, the designated 184-acre Big Flat Laurel Natural Area, has large stands of Pennsylvania's state flower, mountain laurel.

Other maps: USGS topo, McAlevy's Fort quad; Rothrock State Forest map; MSTA map #203; Purple Lizard Recreation map.

Getting there: From US 322 two miles east of Boalsburg, turn right to Tussey Mountain Ski Area. Follow Bear Meadows Road 4.5 miles. Turn right at the 2nd intersection onto North Meadows Road. Drive 2.5 miles up to a "T" intersection with Gettis Ridge Road. About 2 miles up, pause at a roadside vista over Bear Meadows on the left. Then continue to the top and park there.

MAP FOR BIG FLAT, BEAR MEADOWS & JOHN WERT

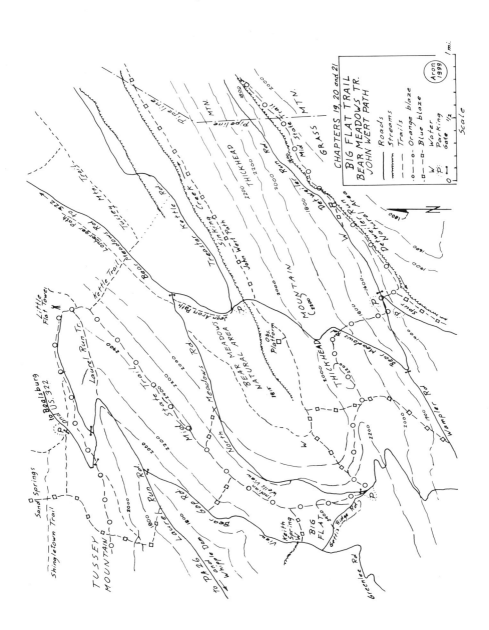

Hike description: Begin the hike on the orange-blazed Mid State Trail to the right (north). This level path cuts through the middle of the Big Flat Laurel Natural Area. The official Pennsylvania state flower predominates here. Besides mountain laurel, huckleberry, chestnut oak, white pine and all the usual community of the ridgetop ecosystem are present.

Follow the orange trail 1 mile, passing the blue-blazed side trail to Keith Spring, and through three charcoal flats, until you arrive at the white rocks, formed of Tuscarora sandstone (400 million years old), which form a natural overlook in an area called Indian Wells. Actual dry "wells" --rounded dugouts in the rock piles -- are found at the far end of the rock field (north side). No one knows who made them nor why. Here you have a superb view to the southeast, over Bear Meadows (a blueberry bog). On the extreme left, if the trees are bare, you may be able to see the tower at Little Flat. You can also look beyond Bear Meadows to Thickhead Mountain, and sometimes Greenwood Firetower on Broad Mountain is visible far away at the righthand side of your view. Close by, a few mountainash trees grow precariously on the rocks at the edge. About September its red-orange berries add spice to your view and attract flocks of cedar waxwings to the feast.

Option #1: If you want to keep your hike very short, you can choose to turn around after seeing the view, and retrace your way 0.3 mile back to the blue-blazed Keith Spring Trail. Turn right. The blue trail goes down about 1/4 mile to the elegant stone basin and piped spring at Bear Gap Road. The stone work at Keith Spring was constructed by the Civilian Conservation Corps around 1934. The marker commemorates Walter J. (Bunny) Keith, a Penn State chemistry professor and inveterate hiker, who spent much time in these mountains.

From Keith Spring turn right and stroll a short way down Bear Gap Road to another overlook. This vista looks northwest across Rudy Ridge and the back side of Tussey Mountain. On the far left you may be able to see the radio tower near PA 26 above Pine Grove Mills.

Now turn around and walk back up Bear Gap Road, past Keith Spring and another 0.2 mile to a road intersection. Straight ahead Greenlee Road continues down towards the Whipple Dam area. You turn left onto Gettis Ridge Road and walk 0.6 mile back to your car. Gettis Ridge Road here is high and level and one of the most colorful places in autumn. When the huckleberry leaves turn red and the trees are orange and yellow, mixed with green pines and an incredibly blue sky, this road is a living rainbow.

Option #2: From Indian Wells View, if you want a slightly longer hike, continue along the ridgetop on the Mid State Trail. In 0.2 mile you reach a signed junction. To the right along the ridge on Mid State Trail, you would reach Little Flat Tower in about 2 miles. But the option #2 short hiker should instead turn left (northwest) at the sign and find the blue-blazed North Meadows Trail. Follow it down steeply 0.3 mile to Bear Gap Road. Turn left and stroll uphill about a mile on this dirt road.

Just before reaching Keith Springs, admire the view to the north across Rudy Ridge. (Check this area carefully for unicorns and other impossibles.) Turn left on the blue-blazed Keith Springs Trail. Then turn right on Mid State Trail and retrace your steps to your car.

For the return trip, you may choose to drive northwest along Gettis Ridge Road. Turn right and drive down Bear Gap Road to Laurel Run Road. Turn right and follow Laurel Run Road back to Galbraith Gap, then turn left on Bear Meadows Road to US 322.

CHAPTER 20
BEAR MEADOWS
Blueberries Are Red When They Are Green

See Map for Big Flat, page 97.

Summary: 3.5 miles; 2 hours walking time; a level circle around
the famous blueberry bog. Rocky or wet in places. Best hiked
during drier periods. The trail is not in the bog, but on somewhat
higher ground, on wide trails and dirt roads, within Rothrock State
Forest and Thickhead Mountain Wild Area.

Location: 7 miles SE of State College. Start from US 322 E.

Features & History: In 1966 Bear Meadows Natural Area was
designated a Registered Natural Landmark because of its
"exceptional value in illustrating the natural history of the U.S."
This 833-acre bog, about 1 mile long and up to 0.3 mile wide, lies
in a fold of the Appalachian mountain ridges. It contains some
plants usually found only in glaciated areas, although the glaciers
never reached here, but stopped about 60 miles northeast. While
not glaciated, the weather conditions were cold and wet. At 1800
feet above sea level, Bear Meadows is a "high altitude boreal
spagnum bog", containing Pleistocene fauna and plants that have
thrived here for 10,000 years, building up a layer of peat 8 ft. thick.

The big highbush blueberries which ripen in August attract many
visitors. Some are four-legged, but most are of the two-legged
variety -- the berry bucket brigades, wearing high boots or old
sneakers, who fill their buckets with "wild blue heaven". If hopping
through wet grass tussocks and knee-deep muck is not your idea of
fun, you may prefer the lower bushes on the drier ground of the
ridges. See Little Flat, Chapter 18. In any case, the blueberry pies,
muffins and pancakes are a great reward.

Note: DCNR official regulations allow gathering edible wild plants "for one's own personal or family consumption." This rules out any berry picking on a commercial scale. Don't be greedy. Please be considerate. Don't pick more than you can eat. Leave some berries for others to enjoy, and especially for the wildlife who may depend on this food source.

Which are blueberries and which are huckleberries? There are 35 different members of the genus, a wide variety of them growing in Pennsylvania on ridges and in bogs, and ripening in overlapping succession from late June through August and into early fall. All are members of the heath family (*Ericaceae*), related to mountain laurel, rhododendron, cranberry, trailing arbutus and heather. According to Bradford Angier's "*Field Guide to Edible Wild Plants*", the blueberry (*Vaccinium*) has numerous soft seeds while the huckleberry (*Gaylussacia*) has 10 stony seedlike nutlets. Some 41 other names for blueberry are listed. None of the tribe is inedible. Beyond that the question is purely academic.

Wildlife thrives at Bear Meadows. You may be entertained by the virtuoso singing of a catbird, and the high trills of marsh-loving redwing blackbirds. You may hear a vireo or a veery. Bullfrogs, woodfrogs, greenfrogs, and peepers vie for attention. Fall colors are especially brilliant in this watery world. The woods contain a mixture of just about every species of tree that grows in Pennsylvania. If the snow is deep enough, this trail can be done easily on cross-country skis. Getting there in winter, however, can be a problem since the roads are not plowed.

Other maps: USGS topo, McAlevys Fort quad; Rothrock State Forest map; MSTA map #203. Purple Lizard Recreation map.

Getting there: From U.S. 322 two miles east of Boalsburg, turn right to Tussey Mountain Ski Area and follow Bear Meadows Road. Bear Meadows Natural Area is exactly 5 miles from the highway. 3.5 miles of the road is paved. You pass three side roads on the way: at 1.4 miles, Laurel Run Road to the right; at 4.4 miles, North Meadows Road to the right; and at 4.9 miles, Treaster Kettle Road to the left. Park at the stone monument with a brass plaque, guarded by a pine tree. Recognize the white pine -- 5 needles in each bundle, soft to the touch. Shake its "hand" and say hello.

Hike description: Walk south across the road bridge. Note the red color of the water which flows out from this acid bog. This is a natural color from the tannic acid of decomposing plant material.

A colony of beavers were active at Bear Meadows from about 1982 to 1986. They built a dam just upstream from the road bridge, which raised the water level in the bog by one or two feet for a 2-year period or more. The beavers moved on, and the blueberry crop of 1986 was reportedly excellent; but there was concern about the survival of some rare bog plants.

Begin your hike on the south side of the bog. Walk past the gate and follow the wide path, keeping the bog on your right.

At the sign "Observation Platform" make a short side trip to the right, walking down through the rhododendrons to the edge of the bog. There, a platform constructed by Centre County CETA in 1978 will give you a closeup look at the bog. You can also look up at the ridge and spot the white rocks of Indian Wells overlook at Big Flat, 500 feet higher than Bear Meadows. See Chapter 19.

Return to the main trail and continue, still keeping the bog on your right, through a mixed hardwood forest. The trail is quite rocky at first, and has deteriorated in places into eroded mud puddles. This is NOT a good choice for bicycles. The Bureau of Forestry has recently posted the trail "NO BIKES". Leave your bikes at home, or park them at the gate to prevent further damage to the Natural Area. Bear Meadows is one of 28 Pennsylvania

Natural Areas designated as special regulation areas for the protection of all amphibians and reptiles.

Along the trail look for dwarf ginseng, goldthread, trillium, Canada Mayflower, and Indian cucumber root. After you have hiked about a mile, you pass the signed, blue-blazed Gettis Trail on your left. The blazes follow your trail for a quarter mile and then depart again to the left. They are part of a loop side trail of the Mid State Trail. You keep going straight ahead, circumnavigating the bog in a clockwise circle.

Just after the blue blazes leave, you will find a spring. This is also called "Sand Spring", though it is no relation to the Sand Spring a couple of miles northwest of here. (See Chapter 7.) Some German hikers have dubbed the spring "*Tuempel*" (little puddle). This spring, and a few others feeding Bear Meadows, form the beginnings of Sinking Creek, which flows northeast through Colyer Lake and Penn's Valley.

Continue into a meadow. There used to be a cabin here, which burned down around 1977. Look around for sun-loving flowers in this open area. A campfire circle makes a handy place to rest. Actual camping here in the Natural Area would be against regulations. Your hike is about half over.

Turn right and follow another old jeep trail for 1.4 miles along the north side of the bog. Pass a gate and emerge on North Meadows Road. Turn right and walk 0.2 mile, passing the signed, blue dot-blazed Lonberger Path on the left.

Just before reaching Bear Meadows Road, turn right at the trail sign onto the Jean Aron Path. This very short trail is a blue-blazed extension of the Lonberger Path, and parallels Bear Meadows Road through the Natural Area. It follows an old grade through hemlock and rhododendron about 0.5 mile to your car at the monument.

CHAPTER 21
THE JOHN WERT PATH
A Ski Trail in July

See Map for Big Flat, page 97.

Summary: 3 miles, 2 hours, shuttle hike; or 6 miles, 4 hours, round trip. The trail roughly follows the right bank of Sinking Creek from its beginnings in the Bear Meadows area to Thickhead Mountain Road above Heckendorn Gap.

Location: 8 miles ESE of State College. Start from US 322 E.

Features: Many x-c ski trails make fine hiking trails. They tend to follow old wagon roads or railroad grades, avoiding much of the steepness (which the hiking purist might prefer), and are just right for the short hiker. This one also offers the coolness of rhododendron tunnels and a splashing stream.

History: The John Wert Path, formerly known as Sinking Creek Trail, was finished in June, 1983, by the Penn State Outing Club's X-C Ski Division. It has been compared to the Alan Seeger Natural Area, and is a similar but wilder version of the same type of rhododendron/ hemlock ecosystem. The path is named for a Centre County man who, as a boy (ca. 1893), accompanied his father along this old wagon road to get timber for their Tusseyville barn.

Other maps: USGS topo, McAlevys Fort, and Barrville quads; Rothrock S. F. map; MSTA map #203; Purple Lizard Rec. map.

Getting there: From U.S. 322, two miles east of Boalsburg turn onto Bear Meadows Rd. Drive 5 miles to Bear Meadows N. A.

Hike description: Walk 100 feet along the road, across the bridge. Look left for a sign and blue dot blazes marking this trail.

There are large hemlocks, white oak, and tulip trees along this trail, but the main feature is the arm-thick rhododendron, twisted into impenetrable thickets, which has minimized human intrusion for many years. Now you may gently intrude, treading softly among the deer signs, while butterflies and dragonflies frolic in the dappled sunlight. Trillium and goldthread can be found growing along the trail. A wood thrush sings; a scarlet tanager is heard, and a peewee calls. There is no need to search for them; they are too well hidden in the canopy. Just listen and enjoy. The lucky and the quiet hiker may be privileged to see a deer, or a porcupine, or even a black bear. The mosquitoes can be vicious near the bog; so whatever else you may forget, remember the insect repellent!!

About 20 minutes down the trail, you reach the first hemlock grove. While not peers of the Alan Seeger giants, these are respectable trees with a circumference of a two-person-hug. The path then bends left to the edge of the water. The reddish brown water does not look appetizing, but it is not human-polluted. That is the normal color of Sinking Creek at this point, since it is full of tannic acid from the decaying plant matter in Bear Meadows bog.

After less than a mile, a double blaze marks a side trail to the left, across a footbridge to a cabin with access to Treaster Kettle Road. A very short hiker can escape this way, completing a left-turn loop by walking back along the roads. The main trail continues ahead and joins an old wagon trail. The walking becomes a bit easier. About 2 miles from the start, your trail crosses the Reichley Trail The old sign may still be hanging there, but without a means of crossing the stream, the trail has not been usable. Looking towards the tea-colored creek you can see the raised, rocky bed of an old logging railroad grade, which closely parallels your path.

In early spring you may hear a raucous quacking sound. Try as you might, you cannot locate any ducks. The racket is coming from some nearby vernal ponds on the right. Closer inspection reveals a convention of pink-skinned wood frogs doing their version of a hot tub party, seemingly intoxicated by the springtime.

After crossing the gas pipeline clearing, the trail continues on the other side and soon passes the first of two hunting cabins. The cabins have stone-lined springs with clear water for canteen refills. Beside the last cabin, your trail is crossed by Shingle Path, a "cross-grain" trail which goes up and down over at least four ridges in three miles. This Path is not marked, but can be located by finding the bridge below the cabin. See Bonus hike below.

The John Wert Path ends at a gate near a sharp bend of Thickhead Mountain Rd. The short hiker's easiest return is the way you came.

If you have two cars, and have planned ahead, you can make it a 3-mile, one way shuttle hike. Leave one car at Bear Meadows. Drive the other car to the other end point, i.e. the sharp bend of Thickhead Mtn. Road. To get there, first backtrack a few hundred feet on Bear Meadows Road. Then turn right onto Treaster Kettle Road. In about 3.5 miles turn right onto Thickhead Mountain Road. Drive about 1 mile to the sharp left switchback. Park near the gate. Begin hiking the trail back towards Bear Meadows.

Bonus: SHINGLE PATH LOOP. For the competent hiker, a longer, adventurous hike of about 7 miles can be devised, using Shingle Path to climb across Little Mountain, cross Treaster Kettle Road and continue to the top of the next ridge, where you turn left on Tussey Mtn.Trail. Follow it back to Kettle Trail, then go down to the right, and cross Bear Meadows Road. Find and follow Lonberger and Jean Aron Paths back to Bear Meadows monument. (*Note: this hike is slightly easier in the reverse direction.*) All of these trails are shown on Map 203 of the Mid State Trail Series. But be advised that most of them receive little or no maintenance. That is what makes the hike so adventurous. Don't try it unless you are confident of your orienteering and trail-finding skills.

CHAPTER 22
DETWEILER NATURAL AREA
Diamonds and Emeralds

Summary: Option #1: <u>2 miles in 1.5 hours</u>. Option #2: <u>4 miles in 3 hours</u>. A short trip through a narrow green valley. Rocks, moss, water and big trees. Rothrock State Forest. Thickhead Mountain Wild Area.

Location: 8 miles SE of State College. Start from US 322 E.

Features: Everything is dark and green in the cool, moist vale. Tiny diamond waterfalls bubble over, around and among the emerald mosses which cushion the rocks. Stately white pines and hemlocks shelter and conceal the secrets of the forest and the rush of joyous water through this hidden glade, where time stands still. You could become a poet.

Although this hike is short, this is definitely not a place to go if you are in a hurry. Much of the trail is extremely uneven and rocky, which enforces a slow and careful pace. Give yourself extra time -- up to twice as much time per mile as you usually need. You will have to watch your feet when you walk, and stop when you look at the scenery. But if you expect and accept this natural speed limit, you will fully enjoy this worthwile gem.

Other maps: USGS topo,McAlevys Fort, and Barrville quads; Rothrock S. F. map; MSTA map #203; Purple Lizard Rec. map. See also *More Outbound Journeys in PA* by Marcia Bonta.

Getting there: From U.S. 322 two miles east of Boalsburg, turn right and follow Bear Meadows Road 7.3 miles. See instructions to Bear Meadows in previous chapter. Beyond Bear Meadows Natural Area, at 5.8 miles from U.S. 322 you cross the summit of Thickhead Mountain. Then the road has two switchbacks going down the south side. At the first switchback at 6.6 miles, Wampler Road goes off to the right (west). You turn sharp left. At the second switchback at 7.3 miles, Detweiler Road, with gate permanently closed, goes off to the left (east) while Bear Meadows Road turns sharp right. Continue a short way and turn off into the parking lot on the right, provided by Rothrock State Forest.

Hike description: Walk back to the Detweiler switchback. Go around the gate and follow the orange-blazed Mid State Trail which descends steeply to the right. This rocky trail is lined with mountain laurel, lushly blooming in June. In 0.1 mile, you'll be down in the vale at the trail junction. To the right, the blue-blazed Greenwood Spur goes through Alan Seeger Natural Area, then over Broad Mountain at Greenwood Firetower and down to Greenwood Furnace State Park, 11 km to PA 305. To the left the orange Mid State Trail goes 16 km to U.S. 322 in the Seven Mountains area; behind you the MST has come 24 km from PA 26.

Turn left and continue following the orange blazes. You will really need your boots (and bless your Vibram soles) on these rough rocks; also bug repellent might be a priority item against the mosquitoes. The trail and Detweiler Run are squeezed between Thickhead Mountain on the north and Grass Mountain on the south. Rhododendrons grace your path and mosses carpet the way. In some spots the roar of the water drowns out all other sounds. When the trail gets farther away from the stream, you are likely to hear the song of the woodthrush. The loud, flute-like "lay-o-lee" is unmistakable and unforgettable.

When you have come about 0.6 mile along the valley trail, you enter the Detweiler Natural Area. No boundary markings are seen, but you will notice some larger trees around you -- oaks, hemlocks and especially white pines. The trail climbs slightly away from the stream. A sandy-bottomed spring emerges near the trail; it is guarded by a white pine over 3 feet in diameter -- a 2-person hug.

MAP FOR DETWEILER, ALAN SEEGER & GRASS MTN.

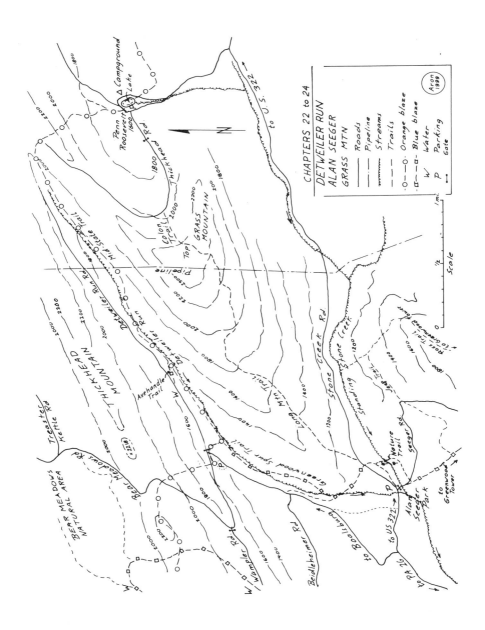

Soon you reach the blue-blazed Axehandle Trail. Option #1 hikers turn left. The Axehandle Trail angles upward and is shaped somewhat like -- well, like an axehandle. After a 5-minute climb the blue trail emerges on Detweiler Road near a spring which has nice stonework of the 1930's Civilian Conservation Corps type. If you did not care to drink at the spring on the trail below, this one may be more potable. Just remember all untreated water is a risk. Option #1 short hikers turn left (west) on the road and follow it 1 mile back to your car.

Option #2 hikers can skip the Axehandle Trail, or come up for a drink and go back down again. Continue following the orange Mid State Trail another mile to the pipeline. The trail becomes somewhat easier, but still rocky, as it follows an old railroad grade. A few rotting ties or their depressions are still visible. Some club mosses are found. Formerly there were three stream crossings, but they have been reduced to one by the addition of a Penn State Outing Club bridge in 1983, and a 1985 Boy Scouts' trail relocation through thick rhododendron.

At the pipeline clearing turn left (north), cross the stream and climb 0.2 mile to Detweiler Road. Turn left (west) on the road and walk 2 miles back to your car.

A third option, if you want to lengthen the hike to about 6 miles, would be to continue on the Mid State Trail for another mile or so. Turn left on the Shingle Path and left again on Detweiler Road. This last section, nearing the upper end of the vale, is even rockier than the rest. It is not well-loved by most short hikers. But if you are growing, give it a try.

After a morning of rock-hopping, even in the timeless beauty of Detweiler, it feels good to stretch your legs on the open road again. It may take about an hour to walk to your car from the pipeline. It should be a relaxed hour. There are no cars on this closed road (but watch for bicycles), no tricky turns, no rocks to trip on. There is time to think, converse with a friend, and enjoy the Earth.

Along the road you may see or hear birds: a hawk, a bluejay, a flicker, a scarlet tanager, an ovenbird, a yellowthroat. You will certainly note the plants and trees. Can you find sweetfern? Sassafras? American chestnut? Striped maple? White birch? In the next chapter, at Alan Seeger, you will meet the great grandfather hemlocks -- giants to be hugged. But here along Detweiler Road you have a chance to meet the young ones. The hemlock loves wet places, so it chose Pennsylvania; and we chose it as our state tree. You can get close and touch the needles, which lie flat along the twigs, like feathers. Hemlocks and the 5-needled white pine are soft and do not say "ouch" when you touch them, as the spruce tree is apt to do.

SUMMER SCENE
(c) Jean Aron 1979

Now deep in the forest the hemlocks are lying
   amid the moist scent of their living and dying.
Rhododendrons are blooming in this cool retreat,
   where a green leafy canopy holds out the heat.

A flashing red tanager warns us to pause,
So we stop, look, and listen, while trees give applause.
The oak tree is king, reaching low, reaching high,
   Grasping deep in the earth, and supporting the sky.

The brook, as it babbles in murmuring tones,
As it tumbles through spillways of moss-covered stones,
   As it dawdles and gurgles and rushes about,
    Sings a lullaby, drowning all other things out.

CHAPTER 23
ALAN SEEGER NATURAL AREA
To Touch a Tree

See map for Detweiler, page 109.

Summary: Part one: <u>half-mile, easy nature trail</u> through the rhododendrons to visit the giant hemlock. Part two: <u>4 miles; 3 hours</u>. Further adventures along Detweiler Run.

Location: 9 miles SSE of State College. Start from US 322 E.

Features: Alan Seeger Natural Area is a special place. You know it the moment you enter the cool deep shade of towering hemlocks. You know it the first time you see the intricately interwoven rhododendrons and admire their annual gift of blossoms. The wind whispers in the high branches and glides through the green tunnels, exalting all it touches. Involuntarily you find yourself walking slowly and reverently through this ancient vaulted "cathedral". In summer Alan Seeger is a cool retreat for a picnic. In July it is worth the trip just to see the rhododendron in bloom. In winter, too, it has a special kind of magic. Fewer people come here then. You will find a snow-cushioned quiet. You may walk the silent paths among curling rhododendron leaves. In cold weather these broad-leaved evergreens like to conserve warmth by rolling their leaves and pretending they are needles. Or you can X-C ski on nearby jeep trails. During trout season, fishermen may find their treasures in Standing Stone Creek and Detweiler Run which flow through the picnic area.

History: The 390 acre hemlock grove was named for a young American poet, killed in France in World War I. It is administered by DCNR Bureau of Forestry. The 1/2 mile nature trail, rebuilt by the Youth Conservation Corps in 1981, is the home of some giant hemlock trees. At least two of them were estimated to be more than 500 years old. It took three people, arms outstretched, to encircle the old great grandfather tree. One giant fell in a storm in May 1982. The other tree was lost in 1996, the last of its generation. New champions may now emerge.

Other maps: USGS topo, McAlevys Fort quad; Rothrock S.F. map; MSTA map #203; Purple Lizard Recreation map. See also, *Outbound Journeys in Pennsylvania* by Marcia Bonta, and *Fifty Hikes in Central Pennsylvania* by Tom Thwaites.

Getting there: There are three ways to get to Alan Seeger:
1) The shortest, most scenic way is to drive across the mountains on Bear Meadows Road. See earlier chapters. 0.7 mile after you pass the Detweiler Road switchback, Beidleheimer Road comes in from the right (west). Continue straight ahead another 1.3 miles. When you reach paved Stone Creek Road, turn left and drive 1/2 mile into the Natural Area. Cross the bridge over Detweiler Run and park near the sign or the picnic shelter. This route is 15.7 miles from State College. It is also the roughest -- dust, gravel, rocks, mountains, and many ways to get lost. Although it is not closed in winter, neither is it plowed of snow.

2) The next shortest way is via PA 26. This route is 20.9 miles from State College, and is the first to be snowfree in spring. Follow PA 26 south through Pine Grove Mills for 14.6 miles. Just before the village of McAlevy's Fort turn left onto Stone Creek Road. Signs may guide you to Alan Seeger from here. After 0.8 mile the road turns right near a farm. After 2 more miles it turns left (unpaved Broad Mountain Road comes in from the right), and in another 0.1 mile it turns right again. When you have driven a total of 6.3 miles from PA 26 you should be in the park.

3)To reach Alan Seeger on paved roads, use the 25.6 mile route via U.S. 322. Follow 322 east through Boalsburg and Potter's Mills for 18.2 miles. When you are opposite the Laurel Creek Reservoir turn right onto Stone Creek Road. Follow it 7.4 miles to the park.

Note: If you return this way, the center barricade in the highway US 322. will prevent you from turning left towards State College. You will have to drive down the mountain to turn around.

Hike description: Begin your walk on the nature trail loop. This is an easy-strolling, shale-covered walkway. Signs help to identify white pine, white oak, shagbark hickory, red oak, red maple, hemlock and rhododendron. To follow it in a counter-clockwise direction: cross the bridge over Standing Stone Creek. (A gate at the bridge closes Seeger Road in winter.) About 0.1 mile up the road turn left onto Alan Seeger Trail. There are four footbridges. The first two, specially designed arched truss bridges, were built by Gert Aron, Penn State Civil Engineering Professor Emeritus, and were installed by a YCC crew in 1996. After you have crossed the two you will come to the remains of the 500 year-old forest monarch -- grandfather hemlock. Climb atop the fallen giant. Did it come down with a thundering crash? Or did it fall silently in the forest with no one there to hear?

Continue on the trail through a rhododendron tunnel, across two more small bridges, which were rebuilt by the YCC in 1982, and may need work again. Reach a trail junction sign which says "Mid State Trail - Greenwood Spur". If you're doing only the short loop, turn left and complete the last 1/4 mile of nature trail to your car.

If you are doing the longer hike, continue straight ahead, following the Greenwood Spur across Stone Creek Road to where the blue-blazed spur turns left on an old railroad grade. Walk through a forest of white oak, maple, birch and young white pines. Soon you reach the John Packard Bridge at the first of four stream crossings on this trail. The former double-log bridge at this site was built by then Mid State Trail overseers, Gert Aron and the late John Packard. It was later dedicated to John's memory. The log bridge has now been replaced by a pressure treated "MST special". This relatively simple design, by Mid State Trail builder, Tom

Thwaites, features one handrail in the middle, and can be installed quickly and cheaply, provided the span is 16 feet or less (20 feet if you can find lumber that long). The earlier log footbridges on the Detweiler Run section of this hike were built in 1985/86 by Penn State Water Resources graduate students.

Much of the spur is close to Detweiler Run, home to a few native brook trout. Just before you get to a cabin, a double blaze alerts you to a turn. The spur then angles to the right across rockier terrain and crosses the Run on a plank bridge, built by the cabin owners. The trail then weaves through a muddy area of pines, hemlocks and fallen trees. You may see a woodpecker or hear a thrush. Cross a small stream on a makeshift log bridge and pass a second cabin; then turn right onto the railroad grade again. Cross Detweiler Run on triple logs. Pass charcoal flats and waterfalls.

1.5 miles from the park the spur joins the orange blazed Mid State Trail. Turn left and climb, a steep but short 0.2 mile to Detweiler Road. Notice that this same piece of trail was only 0.1 mile when you hiked down it in the last chapter. The actual distance is 280 meters or about 14 chains. **TRUTH: All short hikers know that any distance is twice as far going up as it is coming down.**

For the easiest return, turn left on Bear Meadows Rd. Follow it 2 miles downhill; and go left on Stone Creek Rd. 1/2 mile to your car.

Or, for greater adventure, you might want to try a shortcut. After about a mile of walking down Bear Meadows Road, at a place where the road bends to the right, look for an unmarked but obvious, wide grassy trail veering off on the left. For the first half mile it seems like a wonderful old trail, going gently downhill. Then it peters out in a very young forest of white pine seedlings. Don't panic; you are very close to the park. Just keep following the flow of water downhill, tending to the right, and soon see the paved Stone Creek Rd. in the park. Go left, 1/4 mile to your car.

CHAPTER 24
GRASS MOUNTAIN
Scramble Up, Amble Down

See map for Detweiler, page 109.

Summary: <u>4 miles; 3 hours walking</u>. Take 2 cars. Shuttle hike from Penn Roosevelt State Park to Alan Seeger Natural Area. Climb the short but nearly vertical Colon Trail; spend the rest of the morning walking gently downhill. Rothrock State Forest.

Location: 9 miles SE of State College. Start from US 322 E.

Features: The bear went over the mountain, and so will you on this hike. You will almost feel you need ropes or a sky hook on the steepest part; but it is only 1/4 mile up. You can make it somehow. The rest is easy. On the way down you reach a clearing and are presented with a far-reaching vista across rolling hills of field and forest. The distant mists combine with autumn hues, or with a hundred shades of green. In early spring the scene is dotted with ruby buds of maple trees. We call this our vision of "Shangri-la".

This hike can be done in the opposite direction -- walking from Alan Seeger to Penn Roosevelt -- but most short hikers will find it easier to go uphill the shorter distance, no matter how steep, than to sustain an uphill walk for 3 miles.

History: Penn Roosevelt originated in 1933 when the Civilian Conservation Corps set up a work camp during the Great Depression. "Stone Creek Kettle Camp", as it was then called, was one of only 12 African American camps in Pennsylvania. (The CCC of the 1930s was segregated.) Corps members constructed recreational facilities, including the 195-foot dam and many of the surrounding forestry roads and trails. For many years, Penn Roosevelt was a State Forest Picnic Area. In 1983 the 41-acre park was designated a State Park.

Other maps: USGS topo, McAlevys Fort, and Barrville quads; Rothrock S.F. map; MSTA map #203; Purple Lizard Rec. map.

Getting there: To get there drive to Alan Seeger Natural Area. See previous chapter. Leave car #1 there. Drive 4 miles east on paved Stone Creek Road. Turn left on Penn Roosevelt entrance road. It is about 1 mile on gravel to the park. Take the left fork (the right goes to the campground). Park car #2 in the picnic area on the west side of the lake.

Hike description: Begin walking westward up Thickhead Mountain Road. In a little way you pass a gate. Continue up the road for about a mile. The road forms a big horseshoe curve. Where the road levels off, Colon Trail is found on the left at the top of the curve. The trail sign was missing, but the signpost may still be there. The footway of the trail is fairly obvious. The climb starts quite gently, but soon you will see -- trails do not come any steeper. The difficulty is not so much in being short of breath as in just finding enough footholds or trees to grab. Within 15 or 20 minutes, however, everyone should be at the top of this Jacob's ladder. Rest awhile at the charcoal flat under the dead pine tree. The remainder of this hike is a piece of cake.

The trail then continues in a southwesterly direction, across the flat top of Grass Mountain, through thick patches of huckleberries. In places it may be overgrown so look sharp for the footway. In a quarter of a mile it emerges on the pipeline clearing.

Cross the pipeline clearing, heading diagonally to your left (south) and find the wide, comfortable Long Mountain Trail going down. This grass- and moss-covered jeep trail winds gradually down through the woods, passing a few more charcoal flats.

You may see a ruffed grouse, the official Pennsylvania state bird. Usually these small game birds wait until you are almost upon them, and then fly up, in a most startling way, from nearby shrubbery. You see only a squawking brown blur. But sometimes in spring, they may be so involved in courtship rituals they are oblivious to the audience. The male displays his handsome tailfeathers like a peacock, and "drums" the air with his wings. The deep-pitched "drumming" vibrations can be heard, or rather felt, quite far away. Later, in June, if you happen to step too close to a nest, the female may put on a broken-wing show to lure you away from her young.

About 2 miles down, you reach "Shangri-la" vista and a clearcut area. This is often a good lunch stop. The clearing provides a vista for us and a variable habitat and browse for animals and birds. While a mature climax forest may contain tall oak trees and not much else in the understory, clearcutting small areas creates an opportunity for grass, berries and small shrubs to grow, providing more food for wildlife. Snow fence enclosures contain small apple tree seedlings which were provided by the Pennsylvania Game Commission and planted by the Bureau of Forestry as an experiment to grow more food for the animals. Small springs trickle from this area. The trail may be wet, but you may also see some different plant types.

Long Mountain Trail emerges on Stone Creek Road about 1/3 mile northeast of Alan Seeger. Turn right on the road and walk to your car. Or take a softer route via the Greenwood Spur and part of Alan Seeger nature trail. See previous chapter and Detweiler/ Alan Seeger map.

CHAPTER 25
COLYER LAKE
Our Golden Pond

Summary: 3 miles; 2 hours. Around the lake on gentle trails. Colyer is a conservation lake in Centre County, managed by the Pennsylvania Fish & Boat Commission.

Location: 9 miles east of State College. Start from US 322 E.

Features: Colyer Lake is a place for all seasons. In spring a brown thrasher serenades the fishermen. Capricious summer breezes send sailboats flying. Fiery autumn trees admire their reflection in the mirror-still lake. Winter fish in the cold depths below the thick ice listen to the footsteps of ice fishermen and the slice and glide of ice skates. Pink lady slippers and trillium are found by those who love wildflowers. Ospreys find a fish dinner. Woodcocks delight in the bog below the dam. Killdeer cry overhead. Swallows swoop and scoop their meals in flight. A fox sparrow delights an audience of birders, while a phoebe near the bridge bobs its tail and worries. Migrating waterfowl -- ducks, Canada geese, loons, grebes, swans -- all make regular stopovers at this watery wayside inn. Even the mountain stops here. For nearly 100 miles, stretching from the Mason-Dixon Line northward, Tussey Ridge crosses half of Pennsylvania. At last it reaches Colyer and kneels gently at this cozy nugget of a valley.

Other maps: USGS topo, Centre Hall quad; Rothrock S.F. map; MSTA map #204; Purple Lizard Recreation map.

Getting there: From State College take US 322 east less than 10 miles. Turn right at the Colyer Lake sign onto Taylor Hill Road. It is paved, but narrow and winding. Signs guide you to the lake. In 1.25 miles turn right again and go 0.5 mile to the lake's north side parking lot.

MAP FOR COLYER LAKE

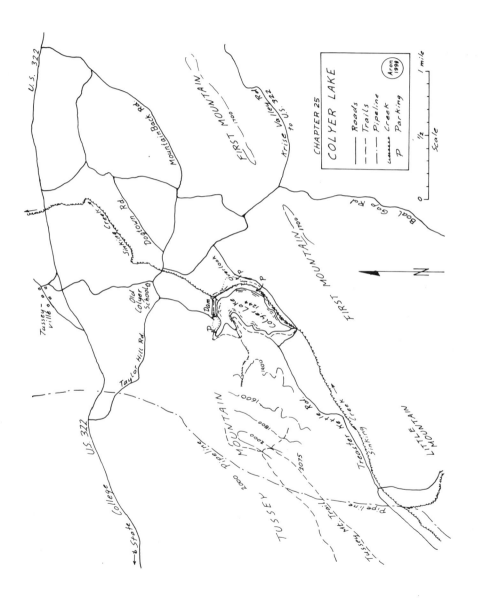

If you miss the first Colyer Lake exit on US 322, there is a second one about a mile farther east, just opposite Tusseyville. If you turn right on this road, drive 0.8 mile to the Old Colyer schoolhouse (converted into a residence), turn right onto the other end of Taylor Hill Road, drive 0.2 mile, then turn left and go 0.5 mile to the north side lot.

Hike description: Before you start your hike, you should walk over to the spillway to check whether the stream is crossable. Because there is no footbridge below the dam, you may not be able to circle the entire lake if the water level is high, fast and furious. You may be able to wade across in warm weather, or cross on stepping stones. In winter, when the lake level is drawn down, you may even be able to walk across on dry or frozen mud above the dam. If in doubt, check it out.

If the stream is not crossable, you can either hike part way around and back, or you can station a second car at the southside parking lot. You get there by driving back out past the schoolhouse corner, turning right at every opportunity. In short it is about 1.75 miles with four right turns to reach the south lot.

To begin your hike from the north side parking lot, you can walk close to the water or choose the bridle/ x-c ski paths somewhat farther away. The latter are generally broader, drier and easier, although they afford fewer views of the lake. The broader paths are described here. Sneakers or good walking shoes are usually adequate footwear, but you might want long pants against the poison ivy and briars.

Start walking on the gated old road going west (away from the dam). There may be interesting meadow flowers along the trail -- note the whorled loosestrife, the spotted knapweed, and yellow St. Johnswort blooming in summer. There are also a few edibles --

wild strawberries, blackberries and wild grapes, which wild critters enjoy. Also notice the poison ivy (three shiny leaves) and the Virginia creeper (five leaves, non-poisonous). Soon the path curves to the left and goes over a hill; you cross a small stream and curve left again. Walk through a plantation of trees -- larch on the left, red pine on the right. The pathway is padded with fallen needles. Soon you find yourself on the south side of the middle inlet, having bypassed the north inlet entirely. You might see pink lady slippers in May, or another interesting wild orchid. A fisherman's path runs close to the water. Look for closed gentian there in September.

The trail then angles up to the right through the pines and meets an old road. To the left the road disappears into the lake. You will turn right along the road; but first walk straight ahead for a view from the promontory. This is a good fall color scene, looking south across the main body of the lake to the south parking lot and First Mountain rising behind it. Sometimes you can spot water birds below.

Follow the dirt road uphill. You have a choice of walking on the narrow cliffside path, which has shade and more views of the water, or the wider road which is safer and easier. When the cliffside path starts to descend toward a small muddy inlet, it is better to go back to the road. The cabin is privately owned, but you can walk a short way down its driveway and cross a small stream Then turn left and find a trail towards the lake again. As you pass the open field, look for bluebird houses on the telephone poles (4 ft. off the ground). If it is nesting season, look around on wires, fences and branches for occupants of the boxes. Tree swallows will also nest readily in bluebird boxes. Listen for frogs among the water lilies in the south inlet or bay, and birds in the field and trees -- a song sparrow, a redwing blackbird a cardinal, a catbird.

Take any path you can find through the tall grass meadow, to arrive on the gravel road (Treaster Kettle Road), and turn left. Check for a phoebe nest under the road bridge. This little brown bird with the tail-bobbing habit likes to nest under bridges or eaves of buildings. Notice the stream coming in here (Sinking Creek) still has some rusty red color from its beginnings in Bear Meadows.

Turn left on the towpath (left bank of the diversion canal). If the path looks too rough, you can walk on the paved road which parallels it. Walk through clover and meadow flowers. Some beaver activity along the canal in 1992 changed the area. Look for signs. The beaver dam is gone now, and the canal is restored. Will the beavers give up trying? Don't count on it.

Continue your hike to the south parking lot. You might want to turn around here and return the way you came. Choosing some alternate paths on the way back makes it quite interesting. For example, if you followed the lake closely on the way out, you might return on the wider, easier roads.

If you are going all the way around, cross the bridge at the south parking lot and turn left on the road for about 0.2 mile to the high overlook parking lot. Near the large staghorn sumac bushes, look for a trail going down to the water. Stay on the right side of the canal and follow it around to the dam. This part is not as well worn and may be overgrown. Walk through tall grasses, knapweed, goldenrod, asters, which may be abuzz with bees. Watch the damselflies and dragonflies in summer -- the fascinating helicopters of the insect world. These are "good bugs". They eat mosquitoes.

When you get to the dam, follow the path down beside the spillway and cross the stream on stones below, or any which way you can. You may take a side trip downstream to look for beaver activity, or woodcock. When you're ready to leave, walk across the dam to the north lot and your car.

CHAPTER 26
CENTRE HALL MOUNTAIN
Green Circle on Top

Summary: 3 miles, 2 hours; This time you can drive to the top of Nittany Mountain, then do a loop walk on woodland trails in Bald Eagle State Forest. The trail is about 3 miles if you use a shuttle on Greens Valley Road , or a 5 mile circle walk, including the road.

Location: 9 miles NE of State College. Start from US 322 E.

Features: Mixed green forest surrounds a small stream with birds and flowers in three seasons. (It is not easily accessible in winter.) Despite some rocks and a wet creek crossing, the trail is mostly flat and inviting to all ages. To shorten the trip, use a shuttle.

A small, isolated chunk of State Forest, lying between Centre Hall and Pleasant Gap, this area surrounds a pretty little creek in its upper reaches on top of Nittany Mountain. The road, the creek and the trails lie in a "saddle" of the mountain, at an elevation of 1700 ft. The ends of the saddle are formed by an 1800 ft. ridge to the northwest, and a taller, 2200 ft. ridge to the southeast. Little Fishing Creek, a PA trout stream, flows from here down through Hecla Gap to Mingoville on PA 64.

History: A keen explorer of these woods might be able to locate parts of the old James Cleveland Trail, built years ago by Boy Scout troops from Centre Hall and Pleasant Gap. Starting from PA 192 on the south side of the mountain, at a private lane 2 miles east of Centre Hall, the trail led up to the site where James Cleveland crashed his mail plane into the mountain back in 1932. In the early 1980s a heavy stone obelisk still marked the crash site. The trail then continued down the north flank, across the creek to Greens Valley Road. *See KTA's "PA Hiking Trails", 9th ed. 1981.*

MAP FOR CENTRE HALL MOUNTAIN

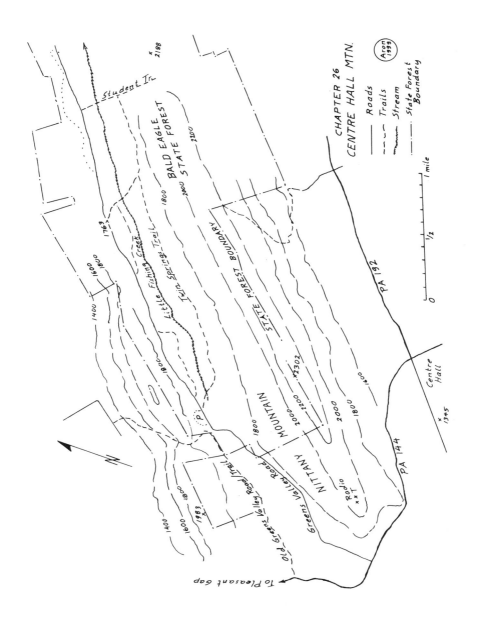

Other Maps: PA Highway map; PA Gazetteer page 62; USGS topo, Centre Hall, and Mingoville quads; Bald Eagle State Forest map.

Driving instructions: From US 322 E. (South Atherton St.) drive through Boalsburg and then east on PA 45 to Old Fort. Turn left on PA 144 and drive through Centre Hall and to the top of the mountain. Just beyond the crest, turn right (northeast) on Greens Valley Road.

(Alternately you can drive to this point from the Pleasant Gap side, using PA 26. Start from East College Ave / PA 26 North, go past Nittany Mall to Pleasant Gap (8 miles). Turn right (southeast) on Route 144 and drive up the mountain. Just before the top, turn left (northeast) onto Greens Valley Road.)

In about 2 miles the pavement ends. State Forest gravel road continues. Park a shuttle car here, if desired, in the parking area on the left. Or drive another 2.5 miles and park near the second sideroad on the right.

Hike description: Begin walking southeast on the sideroad. Cross the small creek (Little Fishing Creek) on stepping stones. Continue until you find a marked trail, where you turn to the right.

Follow Student Trail and Twin Springs or Twin Maples trails, heading southwest paralleling Little Fishing Creek on its south side. These easy old woods trails may or may not be paint blazed. They are not regularly maintained. In about 2.5 miles you should come out to some cabins and to Greens Valley Road where you parked the shuttle car. *If there is no shuttle, turn right and walk along the gravel State Forest road to where you started.*

CHAPTER 27
BLACK MOSHANNON
The Bog on the Plateau

Summary: Moss-Hanne Trail and Star Mill Trail provide a 9-mile, 6-hour long dayhike, using a shuttle; without a shuttle add 2 more miles of road walking for an 11-mile long trip around the lake. The short hiker can shorten it to a 5-mile, 3 hour shuttle hike, or just walk a short way out and back.

Location: 14 miles NW of State College. Start from US 322 W.

Features: 3394-acre Black Moshannon State Park and its 250-acre lake lie atop the Allegheny Plateau. Several small runs collect water from surrounding bogs before emptying into the lake. Wildlife and wildflowers abound. Black Moshannon Bog, a 1592-acre State Natural Area within the State Park, was designated in 1993. The Natural Area, located about 2 miles southwest of the dam, harbors numerous rare plants.

If you've been learning about plants, a whole new world of different flora and fauna opens when you come to the Plateau. Painted trillium, goldthread, common wood-sorrel, bluets, bunchberries and Clintonia dot the forest floor in spring. On a late summer or early fall visit you might see such flowers as closed gentian and ladies' tresses, and be rewarded with the sight of small critters -- a milksnake, a toad, woolybear caterpillars -- as well as deer, ruffed grouse, and even bears. The forest is home to some bird species which generally nest farther north. In winter, the Moss-Hanne Trail makes a good x-c ski trail.

Black Moshannon could be dubbed the Big B -- Bogs, Birds, and Beavers. In August it is Blueberries with a capital B! Allow extra time to graze on the blue bounty of the bushes.

Waterproof hiking boots are recommended on Moss-Hanne Trail. The terrain is level, but often wet and the hike nearly always takes longer than you think. Add time for lunch, rest and looking stops. 5 miles may take 3 hours; or 5 hours, or more. Start early.

History: The word "Moshannon" comes from *moss-hanne*, a native American term meaning "moose stream", the name given to the creek which runs through the park. During the 1800s a lumbering town called Antes was located here. Some of the white pines taken from this area were as large as 6 feet in diameter. The first dam was built by beavers. Later a lumber company built a sawmill dam on the same site. The park was developed in the 1930s by the WPA and CCC.

The Allegheny Plateau geographical region covers about half the state of Pennsylvania. Most of the terrain is gently rolling, soft and high -- very different from the rocky ups and downs of the Ridge and Valley region of central Pennsylvania. The elevation of Black Moshannon Lake is 1865 ft. and the trails you will walk are around 1900 ft.

Other maps: USGS topo, Black Moshannon quad; Moshannon State Forest map; Black Moshannon State Park map; See also: *Fifty Hikes in Central PA* by Tom Thwaites; *More Outbound Journeys* by Marcia Bonta; *PA Hiking Trails, 12th ed.* KTA.

Getting there: The park is located 9 miles east of Philipsburg on PA 504. From State College take US 322 west to US 220. Turn right and drive 1 mile. Turn left just past the Bald Eagle Baptist Church onto Steele Hollow Road. (If you miss this road, there is another in Julian, about 3 miles farther on.) Follow the winding paved road up the Allegheny Front 4.6 miles. At the stop sign turn very sharp left onto the Julian Pike. From here it is another 4 miles to the park.

MAP FOR BLACK MOSHANNON

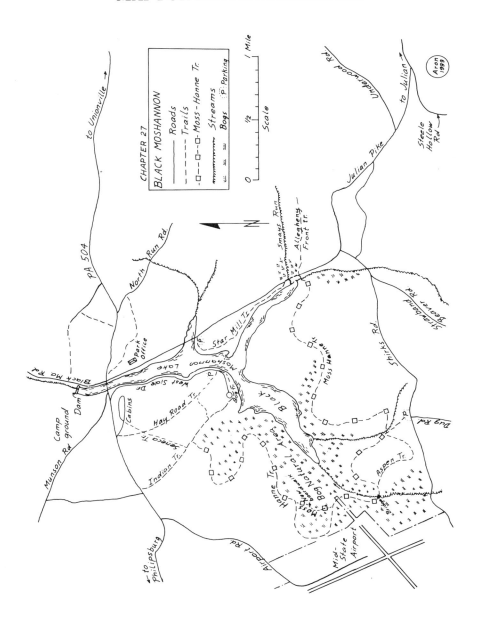

Pick up a park map at the office. Also ask for a Moshannon State Forest Public Use Map for later use; or it can be obtained from the Forest District office in Clearfield, P.O. Box 952, 16830.

To do the 9-mile shuttle hike, park one car on the east side of the lake at Boat Mooring Area 4, located one mile south of PA 504 on the Julian Pike. Or, for the shortened 5-mile shuttle hike, park a car on Shirks Road: 2 miles south of the park office, turn off Julian Pike onto Strawband Beaver Road (west), then right again on Shirks Road and park at the intersection with Dug Road, about 2 miles from the Pike. Then drive the second car back to PA 504; turn left, cross the lake bridge and turn sharp left again onto West Side Road. Park in about 1 mile at Mooring Area 3, near the sign for Bog Trail.

Hike description: Begin your walk on Bog Trail. The 1000 feet of raised wooden walkway and observation deck, built in 1991, are something to brag about. You can walk comfortably and dry shod through the marsh, viewing the lake and the water lilies. Look for the large white flowers of fragrant water lily, the small yellow ones of horned bladderwort and floating leaves of water-shield. You may find the carnivorous sundew plants among the spagnum moss. These resourceful little plants have overcome the bog's short supply of nitrogen by trapping and absorbing insects.

A bog is a wet area with highly acid soil and water, where poor drainage and a cool climate have allowed the buildup of thick mats of plant materials called "peat". The black color of the water is from acids in the decaying plants, including tannic acid--the same substance which makes tea brown. From the platform you can see far up and down the lake, the marshy edges full of water lilies; and tree stumps, birds, and salamanders. You will also see leatherleaf bushes, which grow only in cool, wet acidic conditions; spagnum moss, which has absorbent and antiseptic qualities; and skunk cabbage, the flower with the fetid smell attractive to some insects, if not to us. Notice that the types of plants change as you get farther from the water. Grasses and sedges grow in the wettest part. As they die and build up soil, the area becomes suitable for spagnum moss and leatherleaf. These in turn are succeeded by rhododendron and hemlock trees, which like moist but not wet soil. And finally you find a regular forest of mixed trees on drier soil. During spring wildflower time you may see Clintonia, Indian cucumber-root, Canada Mayflower, painted trillium, goldthread, and starflower.

Back on land, begin following the main trail keeping the lake on your left; pass a plantation of large red pine. Soon Indian Trail joins from the right. When you reach a signed junction of Indian Trail and Moss Hanne, turn left. The trail is paint-blazed with orange triangles which you will follow for the next few hours.

According to a long-time park volunteer who has studied the wildflowers of Black Moshannon, some of the summer flowers you might find are pink lady slippers, wood anemones, purple-fringed orchids, yellow orchids, small white woodland orchids, and Canadian burnet.

After about 2 miles, an area of high-bush blueberries provides sweet snacking on the trail. About 3 miles into your hike you may hear sounds from Mid-State Airport, mostly small private planes now. The controversial National Guard helicopter unit, which used to train here on one weekend each month, has moved away.

Another 800 feet of boardwalk has been constructed, which shortcuts across the marsh on the west side of the park. This new walk, completed in 1995, has moved the Moss-Hanne Trail away from its poor former location along the airport fence, and now provides access to the Bog Natural Area for environmental studies.

About 1/3 mile after crossing an airport approach right of way, you reach another 400-ft. boardwalk and a bridge across the headwaters of Black Moshannon Creek. In 1992 a National Guard helicopter was used to lower the preconstructed footbridge into place, accomplishing the task with very little disturbance to the surrounding bog.

In another mile, after you have passed both ends of the Aspen Trail (an alternate loop), you reach a signed junction. This is an important turn. If you are doing the 5-mile hike, you should have a shuttle car waiting on Shirks Road. Continue straight ahead on the old road grade, and reach that car in a few minutes. If you are doing the 9-mile hike, turn left at the sign and continue following the orange blazes of Moss-Hanne Trail.

In about 1000 feet, the trail passes near a beaver dam and lodge, where industrious critters created a small pool. They were very active in 1992, but may not have survived the deep freeze of the 1993 winter, when the ice was 28 inches thick. Some have moved farther downstream. You may have noticed other, older beaverworks along the trail. This is their kind of country, and they have been around here a long time.

About 8 miles into your hike you emerge on the paved Julian Pike. (If you look across the road, you may notice an orange-blazed trail continuing. That is the Allegheny Front Trail. See next chapter.) Turn left and walk along the road until you can duck into the cool green woods again on the Star Mill Trail. This short 1-mile yellow-blazed trail takes you pleasantly close to the lake shore and avoids most of the traffic from the cottages. Don't miss the left turn onto the relocated part of the Star Mill Trail.

Your hike ends at Boat Mooring #4, where a lakeside picnic table and a restroom offer comfortable waiting while you shuttle the cars.

CHAPTER 28
ALLEGHENY FRONT TRAIL
A New Outlook

Summary: From Julian Pike in Black Moshannon State Park, option # 1 is a 6-mile, 5-hour one way shuttle hike along the rugged up and down edge of the Allegheny Plateau; option #2 is a less rugged, 6-mile, 3-hour out-and-back trip to see a new vista; option #3, 1-mile, 1-hour, just out to the new vista and back from Underwood Road, a dirt forestry road.

Other hiking options abound along the 45 + total miles of this great new circle of trails through Moshannon State Forest, surrounding Black Moshannon State Park. Particularly nice sections of Allegheny Front Trail can be found on the north side along Benner Run, and on the west side along Six Mile Run. The great circle also incorporates sections of Rock Run Trail, and Moss Hanne Trail in Black Moshannon State Park. See chapters 27 & 29. An AFT map is available from Moshannon State Forest Office, Box 952, Clearfield, PA 16830. Phone: 814-765-0821.

Location: 12 miles NW of State College. Start from US 322 W.

Features: Even the shortest option involves some dexterity in getting down through some interesting rocks. But it is worth the trip to get to "Ralph's Majestic View". On a clear day you can see "the whole world" from here. Gazing southeast from an elevation of 2200 ft., this overlook shows you parts of Nittany Valley and Tussey Mountain on the horizon. A few water towers, domes or radio towers may be visible, but most of the civilization in State College is hidden behind Bald Eagle Ridge in the mid-distance and the bumpy hollows of the Front tapering off just below you.

The trail along The Front is rougher than you might expect. The Allegheny Plateau does not end abruptly, but presents a jagged, indecisive edge. The "edge" may be 3-or 4-miles wide, where the land drops, gradually and unwillingly, from the heights above 2000 ft. to the valley floor around 1000 ft. above sea level. There are no large bluffs or cliffs. Ancient streams have carved and worn myriad small valleys into the Front and piled up small hills below it. The terrain is rolling and rocky. The hiker is constantly going up, down, and around side stream cuts. When you are at the highest points, you are not at the edge. If you try to go to the edge, you will be far down the hill. Both the challenge and the beauty and charm of this geologic boundary make it well worth the effort.

History: A grand scheme for a trail running along the whole length of the Allegheny Front, from Prince Gallitzin State Park to Bald Eagle State Park, was first envisioned by Larry Pittis, a member of Appalachian Mountain Club. This long-distance hiking trail was to be called "Lost Mountain Trail". The idea was advanced to Keystone Trails Association in 1994 and 1995. Although interesting, the idea was not very practical, since Pittis was not a resident of Pennsylvania, and could not muster enough volunteer labor and support.

Actual development of a trail, was left for another inveterate trail builder, Ralph M. Seeley, a Penn State University retired Associate Professor of Engineering Research. Working with personnel from the Moshannon District Bureau of Forestry and Black Moshannon State Park, Seeley enlisted the help of Penn State Outing Club, Ridge and Valley Outings Club, and KTA's TrailCare Team, to explore, lay out, and build a big circle of trails. Since the first section was along the edge of the Allegheny Front on the proposed route of the Lost Mountain Trail, it was decided to call this new trail system "Allegheny Front Trail". Work was begun in the fall of 1995. The 26-mile eastern loop was completed in 1997, and the western loop in 1998 to 1999, making a circle of over 45 miles.

MAP FOR ALLEGHENY FRONT TRAIL

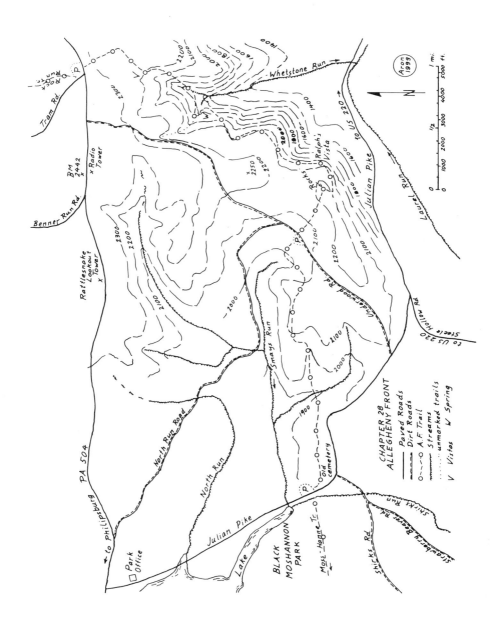

In October, 1998, Ralph Seeley was honored with the first-ever
Conservation Volunteer of the Year Award by PA Dept. of
Conservation and Natural Resources, for his work over two
decades, in planning, building, and maintenance of hiking and x-c
ski trails, and footbridges. Since 1981 he has put in over 6000
hours of labor into trails, mostly in the Moshannon District.
Perhaps more importantly, he has encouraged and guided
innumerable other people to become involved in the enjoyment and
maintenance of these resources. He has developed a system of
volunteer overseers for this trail, as well as Rock Run Trail and
parts of Quehanna, which you will follow in later chapters. We all
owe a huge debt of gratitude to the leadership of a small, quiet,
unassuming man, who has done a giant-sized job.

Other maps: the KTA book, *PA Hiking Trails*, 12th ed. 1998;
Moshannon State Forest map; Black Moshannon State Park map;
USGS topo / Black Moshannon, and Bear Knob quads; PA
Highway Map; PA Gazeteer, pg. 61.

Getting there: Start from US 322 West / North Atherton St.
Follow instructions to Black Moshannon State Park (previous
chapter). Just before reaching the Park, if you are doing the
shortest option #3 hike, look for Underwood Road. It is on the
right (north) from Julian Pike, 1/2 mile west of the intersection with
Steel Hollow Road. Turn right. Drive about a mile on the rough
dirt road. Park near the orange-blazed trail crossing.

For option #2 or #1, continue on Julian Pike 1 more mile, and
park along the paved road. Look for a sign identifying Moss Hanne
Trail on the (west), and orange blazes on both sides of the road.

If you are doing the 6-mile, out-and-back option #2, your trail
starts here on the right (east) side. Just follow the blazes 3 miles to
the view from the Front, and return the same way.

If you are doing the shuttle option #1, the whole 6-mile Front, leave one car here at Julian Pike, and continue driving another mile to PA 504 (Rattlesnake Pike), turn right (east) and drive 5 miles to the trailhead parking on the north side of the road. This small gravel lot near Tram Road serves both AFT and Rock Run Trail.

Hike Description: Cross the highway (PA504) and find the rectangular orange blazes on the south side. Don't confuse the trail blaze with other markers for snowmobile trails. You will be following this orange blaze the whole way, as the AFT seeks to follow old trails and grades along the scalloped edges. After going part way down into a hollow it may then climb back up again, traversing to another vantage point.

In 1 mile you reach a vista above Whetstone Run, which looks south to the end of Tussey Mountain. The trail then drops down the eastern arm of Whetstone Run and back up again on a log slide path, reaching a spring in another half mile. (A steep, rough side trail continuing up the log slide can provide an emergency intermediate access from Underwood Road.) The orange AFT leaves the logslide path and continues southwest.

About 3 miles from the start, you reach "Ralph's Majestic View", one of the main features of this hike, described earlier in this chapter. From here it is a short scramble up through a rock outcropping, then an easy half-mile hike through young woods to Underwood Road, where Option #1 hikers start and end their hike.

The easier second half of the trail, from Ralph's Majestic View to Julian Pike, is the part Option #2 hikers will do as an out-and-back.

Continue carefully following the blazes, which will take you away from the edge, through the gentler, rolling terrain of the plateau. Cross an arm of Smay's Run, some interesting boggy areas, and across "one more hill, children", and reach your car at Julian Pike.

CHAPTER 29
ROCK RUN TRAIL
Quality Time

Summary: A wild trail, but improving. Choose a hike: from 5 miles/ 3 hours walking time on the shortest loop; to 13 miles/ 7 hours walking the entire trail, or stretch it into a 2-day easy beginner's backpack.

Location: 14 miles NNE of State College. Start from US 322 W.

History: Exploring and cutting of Rock Run Trail was begun in 1982 by the Penn State Outing Club X-C Ski Division. You can help with maintenance of these trails. To become an overseer, or to obtain more information about Rock Run Trail, call PSOC Advisor Ralph Seeley at 814-692-8223 or write to 2025 Halfmoon Valley Road, Port Matilda, PA 16870.

Features: An isolated forest place surrounding a wild trout stream, the 13 miles of foot trail centered around Middle Branch Rock Run, roughly form a figure eight. A short hike on either of the loops, or a longer all day or even 2-day hike of the entire trail will take you into a world of natural quiet. Depending on the season, you may glide on skis through the silence; or enjoy the varied songs of a hundred warblers and the crimson flash of a scarlet tanager; observe wild trout spawning, the white tails of shy deer; the powerful blooming of rhododendron and mountain laurel; the fiery autumn woods; the rush of cool waters. Whatever else you find at Rock Run, the time you spend here with friends or family will be remembered as Quality Time.

Other maps: Rock Run Trails map from DCNR Bureau of Forestry; Moshannon State Forest map, or Penn State Outing Club map. See also: *PA Hiking Trails,* KTA, 12th ed. 1998; *Fifty Hikes in Central Pennsylvania*, by Tom Thwaites.

MAP FOR ROCK RUN

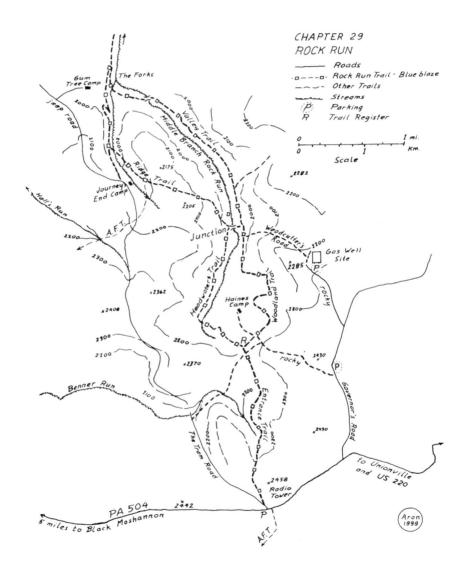

CHAPTER 29
ROCK RUN

———— Roads
-□--- Rock Run Trail - Blue blaze
-⌒- Other Trails
⌒⌒ Streams
P Parking
R Trail Register

Getting there: Rock Run Trail is located about five miles northeast of Black Moshannon State Park, off PA 504. Follow instructions in the previous chapter to Black Moshannon State Park. At the intersection of Julian Pike and PA 504 in the park, turn right (east) and drive about 5 miles. Rock Run Trail lies about two miles north of PA 504. The main trail, figure-eight-shaped, has a 5-mile northern loop comprised of Ridge Trail and Valley Trail, and a 3.5-mile southern loop comprised of Headwaters Trail and Woodland Trail. There are three "entrance trails", ranging in length from 0.7 mile to 2 miles (double that for a round trip); all connect to the southern or upstream loop, on the southeastern leg of the figure eight, called Woodland Trail. The most easily accessible entrance is also the longest (2 miles). The shortest entrance trail (0.7 mile) requires driving on a rocky road. Choose your poison.

Here are the three options:

1) The official Entrance Trail begins just off PA 504 at Tram Road, 5 miles east of Black Moshannon, at a new, graveled, trailhead parking area. Allegheny Front Trail crosses the road here. This is the only Rock Run entrance from a paved road, which is important in winter. This trail was specially cut in 1985 to provide access to Rock Run. Follow it 2 miles, over a hill and across a stream, to a signed junction with Rock Run Trail at its southernmost point. Please sign the trail register in the mailbox.

2) To reach the second entrance: from Tram Road drive another 0.7 mile east on PA 504. Just before leaving State Forest, turn left (north) and drive one mile on the wide, graveled Governor's Road, formerly known as Snow Shoe Road or Game Commission Road. Near the heighth of land, look on the left for a trail sign and a rough, camp road. Park on the roadside. The rough road leads to two or three hunting camps, and is not blazed. Follow it 1 mile across the high plateau, and descending until it crosses Rock Run Trail. Look sharp for the sign and the blue blazes where it crosses the Woodland Trail (southeastern leg of Rock Run Trail). To the

left it is 0.2 mile to Entrance Trail. To the right it is 1.5 miles to the third entrance (Woodcutter's Road).

3) To reach the third entrance, and do the shortest hike, drive another half mile on Governor's Road (total 1.5 miles from PA 504). Turn left on a rough road with fist-sized gravel. Drive down this rocky way 0.6 mile to a clearing, where the road is blocked by a stone pile. Park on the right. Continue walking down the road another 0.1 mile past a gas well site, then turn left passing some boulder barricades, and walk gradually downhill on a jeep trail called Woodcutter's Road. In 0.7 mile you reach the signed, blue-blazed trail.

Hike description: To continue your hike, turn right on Woodland Trail, following an old tramway. Soon you reach another signpost and more blazes, all blue.

At the signpost you have two choices:
1) To do the 5-mile northern loop keep to the right in a northerly direction. Valley Trail goes downstream and offers flowers, birds, birches and a good footbridge. The return on Ridge Trail follows an easy tramway with switchbacks, and some nice campsites under hemlock trees. The northern loop has one or two hills which the very short hiker might notice.

2) To hike the shortest, 3.5-mile southern loop keep to the left at the signpost. Follow the trail down to the stream and across a bridge to the Junction, an area where the two loops join. Again keep left on Headwaters Trail in a southerly direction, around the headwaters of Middle Branch Rock Run. The hike takes you near splashing brooks, springs and tiny waterfalls, through mixed woods and mountain laurel, passing Entrance Trail (where the trail register box is located) and the second entrance, (where Woodland Trail crosses the long camp driveway) until you reach Woodcutter's Road again. Retrace your steps, uphill going out, to your car.

CHAPTER 30
GREENWOOD FURNACE
A Charcoal Sketchbook

Summary: The Tramway and Collier Trails at this State Park can be part of a <u>4-mile, 2-hour</u> loop through the woods on relatively flat trails requiring no special ability--only comfortable shoes. You may opt to extend your hike to cover the entire Ore Banks Loop, making it <u>5.9 miles in 3 hours</u>. Additionally, two other "*bonus hikes*" are described briefly. Both leave from the park and are about 4 miles each. Hiking boots are recommended for these.

Location: 12 miles SE of State College. Start from PA 26 S.

Features: The 423-acre park includes a 6-acre lake, and provides swimming, fishing, picnicking and camping in addition to varied hiking opportunities. A trip to Greenwood Furnace is an informative field trip into the history of early Pennsylvania ironmaking. The self-guiding displays along the trails are a good outdoor museum on the subject of charcoal making. A new indoor museum, the restoration of historic sites, and regular programs for the public, including guided walks on some of the trails, have transformed this small state park into an important educational resource, and a first class park. In the future it may also become a major trailhead. The Link Trail, and a spur of Mid State Trail begin here. Besides the trails which are described, there are plans for clearing several other hiking and x-c ski trails to radiate out from this "trail hub".

Other maps: PA Highway map; PA Gazetteer, page 62; USGS topo, McAlevys Fort quad; Rothrock State Forest map; Purple Lizard Recreation map; Greenwood Furnace State Park map; Brush Ridge X-C Ski Trail map, by DCNR Rothrock State Forest.

MAP FOR GREENWOOD FURNACE

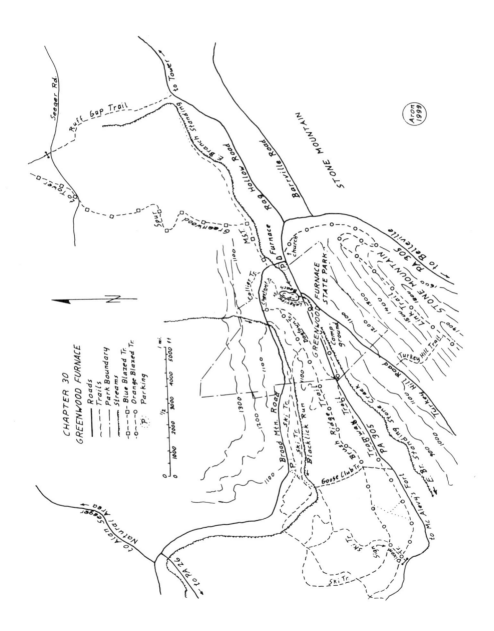

Getting there: Follow PA 26 South 15 miles to McAlevy's Fort. Continue on PA 305 east about 5 miles to Greenwood Furnace S.P. Leave your car in the lot near the park office. Pick up a park map.

History and Hike description: Begin your hike with a history lesson at the Furnace Stacks, located about 500 feet northeast of the office. Greenwood Iron Furnace operated from 1833 to 1904, and used both the cold blast and hot blast processes of ironmaking. The Tramway Trail, which you will hike later, was used to haul raw iron ore to the furnace site, using mule-drawn tramcarts. After viewing the Furnace Stacks, if time permits, you can follow the way eastward to check out some other historic sites: the Company Meat House, the Ironmaster's Mansion, and Mansion Stables. Just across the highway is the old Church. (The northern terminus of the Link Trail is also there. Information about this 72-mile long-distance hiking trail can be obtained from Keystone Trails Association, P.O. Box 251, Cogan Station, PA 17728.)

Bonus hike #1: Link Trail loop *on Stone Mountain.* <u>*4 miles, 2 hours;*</u> *rated moderately difficult because of the rocks and steepness. Start at the signed trailhead near the old Church on PA305. Follow the orange-blazed trail, beginning on the old Belleville Wagon Road, and winding gradually up to the top of Stone Mountain. Continue heading southwest, enjoying views along the mountain top for about 1 mile. Find and turn right on the Turkey Hill Trail, which drops down, steeply at times, reaching Turkey Hill Road in half a mile. Turn right on the road and follow it 1 mile to the park.*

To continue the main hike from the Furnace Stacks, head north on Broad Mountain Road (formerly Black Lick Road). After crossing the bridge, notice the sign and blue blazes on the right which mark the Greenwood Spur of the Mid State Trail. For the more ambitious, a 6.5 mile hike begins here -- 3 miles uphill to the Greenwood Fire Tower, and back on other trails. This hike is described in Tom Thwaites' "*Fifty Hikes in Central Pennsylvania*". A left turn at the same sign brings you to the Museum and Visitors' Center on the site of the old Wagon and Blacksmith Shop, which is another worthwhile stop, if there is time. Check out their displays, see the video, shop the bookstore. Restrooms are located nearby.

To begin hiking the Collier Trail, continue north on Broad Mountain Road and find more information at each guidepost: (5)The Boarding House; (6)The Paymaster's House. After the road curves to the left, leave it and look on the right for the Collier Trail and (7)The School House. Follow the trail past (8)The Woodchoppers; (9)The Collier Hut; (10)The Greenwood Forest; (11 & 12)The Charcoal Mound. *Note: There are plans to rebuild and relocate some of the interpretive trails. Look for changes.*

Cross Broad Mountain Road again and continue on Chestnut Spring Trail, which leads around a hill and back into the picnic area, emerging at Pavilion #1, which has its back pressed against the hillside. If you are skipping the Collier interpretive trail, you can start your hike here.

Hike description: Begin walking on the Lakeview Trail, which skirts around the west side of the 6-acre lake. The beach area is on the other side of the lake. The "beech" area is on this side. Beech trees, growing here are easy to identify in spring by their smooth gray bark, long cigar-shaped buds and the yellowed, oval leaves still clinging to the branches in March. Follow Lakeview Trail around to the dam.

Cross the highway cautiously, and look for the path heading downhill to your right. There you will find an archeological dig at (13)The Grist Mill, and a sign with a routed figure of a mule and tramcart identifying the "Tramway Trail". Proceed west on this easy trail which runs parallel to the highway for 3/4 mile. Look for tulip trees and some Christmas fern, so called because of the stocking-shaped leaflets.

Soon you arrive at a major crossing, where the Tramway Trail crosses PA 305, and a snowmobile route called Dogtown Trail, and the old park boundary all at one spot. You may shorten your hike by using the snowmobile route, if there is no snow.

The second section of the Tramway Trail, continues to run parallel to the highway on the other side. Much of this section still shows impressions in the footway where railroad ties once lay.

The trail passes north of a cabin (Green Brush Camp), and continues in a westerly direction for another mile or two. *If you are still long enough on time and energy, and want to do the entire 5.9-mile "Ore Mine Loop" which was recently cleared, you can continue following orange-blazes on Tramway Trail until they turn right on Dixon Trail, and go up to meet Brush Ridge Trail. They then turn right again and follow Brush Ridge and Chestnut Spring Trails back to the park. This would probably add about an hour to your hike. You would see remains of some ore banks located beyond the Goose Club Trail.*

To follow the original short 4-mile hike, look for the first definite cross trail about 0.3 mile beyond the cabin. The Goose Club Trail may have a yellow blaze. Turn right and go uphill shortly (100 feet of rise), and then turn right again on the Brush Ridge Roadtrail.

This unimproved dirt road follows the top of a low ridge (1200 feet). In winter and early spring you have views through the bare trees. To your right (south) is Stone Mountain. Rising to your left (north) is Broad Mountain, where Greenwood Fire Tower is located. Beyond Broad Mountain you can see Tussey Mountain.

After about 1.5 miles going eastward on Brush Ridge you pass a quarry. You are getting close to the lake and might even catch a glimpse of it if you walk over to the edge of the quarry area. The snowmobile trail comes in from the right (south) at the corner, where Brush Ridge Roadtrail bends to the left (north). 0.1 mile after the bend, you come out on Broad Mountain Road (formerly Black Lick Rd.). Turn right on Chestnut Spring Trail It is 0.2 mile to the Park.

Bonus hike: Black Lick Hike*. 4 miles, 2 hours. Streamside trail through cool, moist hemlock and rhododendron vale, located just north and west of Greenwood Furnace Park. From Greenwood Furnace S.P. begin on Chestnut Spring Trail; follow it north and west & turn left onto Brush Ridge Roadtrail. Pass a gate and hike up the Roadtrail about half a mile, then turn right at a "Ski Trail" sign onto the first old grade heading down at a northwest angle to the Run. Cross a bridge over the upper (east) end of Black Lick Run. Follow the blue-dot marked trail going downstream. In about a mile, you reach Goose Club Trail. Turn left, cross the stream, and climb the hill, keeping left on the Goose Club Trail. At the top, turn left on Brush Ridge Roadtrail, and follow it and Chestnut Spring Trail about 2 miles back to the Park.*

Note: a number of other trails can be found in this area. It can be very interesting to explore them, but confusing. Take good maps and compass, and be prepared to get lost. We did, but only for 10 minutes. If you like the challenge, try it -- on your own.

Black Lick Run Trail is part of Brush Ridge X-C Ski Trail system, built in 1995 by a PCC crew working with Rothrock Forest District. Two x-c ski loops -- the easy 2.2 mile Black Lick Run Loop, and the difficult 5 mile Brush Ridge Loop -- both leave from a new State Forest parking lot, located about 2 miles from Greenwood Furnace S.P. off Broad Mountain Road. (a.k.a. Black Lick Road) Call 814-643-2340 to obtain a map.

CHAPTER 31
MARTIN GAP/ ROCKY RIDGE
Heaven in May

Summary: This <u>3-hour, 3.5-mile loop</u> takes you through flower sprinkled open woods and to the top of a low ridge, past a series of towering, water-scoured boulders in a State Forest Natural Area.

Location: 15 miles south of State College. Start from PA 26 S.

Features: The wildflowers of Martin Gap reach an ecstatic peak of glory in May, but the whole family will enjoy this hike anytime. Exploring the rock formations is like climbing on the backbone of a reclining giant, and requires a fair amount of dexterity. The pock marked monoliths, twisted and jumbled into a natural sculpture garden of fantastic shapes, dominate the area. The main trail leads through the middle of some of these stony havens, and you may opt to explore others on your own. If nimbleness is *not* your forte, these castle walls can easily be bypassed by walking on a gentler trail just below, while others scramble through the rock jungle gym.

History: The Martin Gap area, in Rothrock State Forest in Huntingdon County, has long been recognized by teachers and naturalists as a diverse outdoor learning lab. The primary features are the Oriskany sandstone outcroppings, and an unusual diversity of plant types, including a few wildflowers that are rare to Pennsylvania. This diversity reflects the presence of many different soil types. In 1988 it was proposed (by yours truly) as a State Natural Area. The campaign was soon joined by a diverse array of conservationists, wildflower lovers, birdwatchers, geologists, and outdoor enthusiasts. After many letters, visits, and expert opinions, about 150 acres, or half of the proposed acreage, was officially designated a Natural Area. The listing was published in the Pennsylvania Bulletin on September 18, 1993, as "Rocky Ridge Natural Area", one of a group of eighteen new Pennsylvania

Natural Areas. Although many would have preferred the name "Martin Gap N.A." it is rewarding to know we helped to save an uncommon piece of Penns Woods for everyone to enjoy.

Rocky Ridge Natural Area is shown on the new Rothrock State Forest Map. (Rev.8-98) The boundaries extend along Frew Road from Martin Gap to the powerline, and along a timber haul road on the western side of Rocky Ridge. The northern part, as a Natural Area, will never be logged. The southern part from the powerline to the end of Frew Road was placed under "special management", meaning that any logging would be done selectively about once every 30 years.

Other maps: PA Highway map; PA Gazetteer, page 62; Rothrock State Forest map. KTA's Link Trail maps and guide. See also *More Outbound Journeys in PA* by Marcia Bonta.

Getting there: Start from West College Ave.; follow PA 26 South about 20 miles, passing through McAlevy's Fort. At the Saulsburg road sign, near a white church, turn left (south) onto Martin Gap Road. After a mile, cross the bridge over Standing Stone Creek and keep right. Follow a dirt road into Rothrock State Forest and pass a shale pit and a pair of rustic log cabins. Where the road forks, keep right and follow Frew Road. After half a mile, find a small parking area on the left. Park your car here. It is just a short way beyond this where the orange-blazed Link Trail (gated on the east side) crosses Frew Road. Do not park at the trail and block the gate. There is a stiff fine for blocking emergency access.

The Link Trail is a 72-mile hiking trail, laid out by Keystone Trails Association in 1981 to 1985. It links the Tuscarora Trail near Cowan's Gap State Park with the Mid State Trail system at Greenwood Furnace State Park. For more information on the Link Trail write to Keystone Trails Association, P.O. Box 251, Cogan Station, PA 17728.

MAP FOR MARTIN GAP

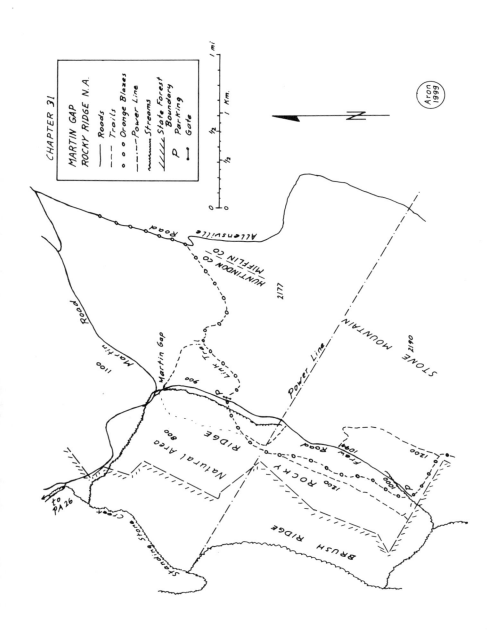

Hike description: From the road crossing, begin following the rectangular orange blazes to the right (west side) down to and across a small stream. Look for white, yellow, and common violets; hepatica; rue anemone; and fringed polygala. Closer to the stream find Jack-in-the-pulpit; bishop's cap, maidenhair fern, wild ginger; and, if you are really blessed, showy orchis. A rare species, puttyroot *"Aplectrum hyemale"*, can also be found here.

Note: wildflowers belong in the woods. Picking them would be stealing enjoyment from others. It is illegal and UNTHINKABLE!

The stream has been swallowed by a sinkhole just above the trail crossing. The water has gone underground, so the streambed is often completely dry. On the other side the blazes angle up a series of switchbacks to the top of the ridge. The 300 ft. rise can be a significant climb for a short hiker. But there are plants to see and birds to hear. Part way up you may chance upon some yellow lady slippers. Squawroot is usually found here, too. A red-bellied woodpecker gives a giggling, tickly sort of call. Various warblers move through the trees. Take your time going up. It is worth the trip. We once encountered a box turtle coming up the trail even more slowly than we.

Rocky Ridge consists of a sentinel row of large, eroded sandstone fortresses of jumbled rock. These form the backbone of this leading ridge (1200 feet elevation) which stands between the valley of Standing Stone Creek and the 2100 ft. high Stone Mountain east of it. At about the 1100 ft. level, on the ledge east of the rock formations, there is a series of large sinkholes at regular intervals along the ridge. The difference between this more alkaline layer and that of the more acidic Oriskany sandstone 100 feet higher is demonstrated by the differing plant communities.

On the ridgetop the trail winds through the rocky bones of the mountain. The rectangular orange blazes show the way. Unless you are are handicapped or very young or very old, everyone should experience crawling through the boulders at least once. You will need all four limbs and a reasonable flexibility and balance. The experience puts you literally in touch with the earth, and close to the sky. If you would rather skip this part, just turn left and follow the orange circle blazes along an easy path at the base of the rocks. At the powerline turn right and walk up to meet your dexterous friends when they come out of the rock pile.

Another day, if more rock scrambling is wanted, try exploring the north end of Rocky Ridge. You can leave the blazed trail and make your own way back towards the Gap. You may discover some new, previously unknown feature in the Natural Area. When you run out of ridge, a steep trail on the east side descends to the junction of Martin and Frew Roads.

Today, if you are following the blazes, stop at the powerline clearing. Look for ant lion pits in the sand under the rock overhang. If you probe these small depressions, which look like they were made by dripping water, you may locate the critter who made it. They are neither ants nor lions, but rather an insect with a taste for ants. Having hollowed out a pit, the ant lion burrows into the bottom to await the misfortune of a passing ant who gets trapped on the slippery slopes of a little sand funnel.

One rock at the powerline is crowned with a seldom seen flower -- pale corydalis, *Corydalis sempervirens*. The leaves resemble wild bleeding heart. The flowers, which bloom in summer, are pale pink with yellow lips. Just past the powerline a bower of pink lady slippers nestles near the base of the rocks.

Now outside the Natural Area, the trail continues southwest, veering left across the sinkhole layer, and then heading downward. Delicious morel mushrooms and more yellow lady slippers might be found. The more astute may discover some *Obolaria virginica* or pennywort, a tiny member of the gentian family, which is rare in Pennsylvania. Enjoy the dogwood in bloom; more rue anemone; pussytoes; gill-over-the-ground; Mayapple; Solomon's seal; and the droopy yellow flowers of perfoliate bellwort. Birds and butterflies may entertain you. You may encounter a resident black rat snake -- startling but harmless. You might also encounter a timber rattlesnake, which is not so harmless, but quite rarely seen. They are not aggressive, and will stay hidden if they hear you coming. Be sensibly alert and cautious to the possible presence of rattlers; watch where you put your feet and hands; but do not let an unreasoning fear spoil your enjoyment. They are pretty special.

After you cross a second small stream, find Frew Road again where it ends in a gravel parking area at the boundary of private land. From here it is an easy going, 1.4-mile roadwalk back to your car (unless you have cleverly left a 2nd shuttle car here). Watch for more wildflowers and birds as you return along the road; check for indigo buntings at the powerline. You may even see signs of bear. Don't worry. Pennsylvania black bears are shy. If you see one, just give him a wide berth. He probably wants to avoid you, too.

At first the waterway is flowing southwest. After passing the high point, another stream flows northeast. And it is all downhill.

Bonus side trip: *Visit the new Stone Mountain Hawk Watching Platform. A very civilized wooden platform was constructed atop the rocky mountain ridge in 1996 or 1997 by folks from the local birding clubs: State College Bird Club and Juniata Valley Audubon Society. A 15 minute walk across the short, but extremely rocky trail from Allensville Road will get you there.*

Leaving Martins Gap, turn right on Martin Road and drive up the mountain. Turn right again on Allensville Road and continue to the top. Park at the crest of the mountain (the county line). Follow a cleared path left (north) along the ridge, soon joined by the orange Link Trail, which takes you to the Platform.

CHAPTER 32
COLERAIN PARK
Wildflowers, Ice Caves and Lookouts

Summary: <u>4 miles; 3 hours walking time</u>. Part one: 1/2 mile wildflower walk along the creek; return the same way. Part two: Climb a steep switchback trail, about 3/4 mile up to Indian Lookout; spectacular views. Easy return on a forestry road with more views and flowers.

Location: 17 miles SW of State College. Start from PA 26 S.

Features: Colerain is a small State Forest Picnic Area nestled between Tussey Mountain and Spruce Creek, the trout stream made famous by the visits of President Jimmy Carter. An interesting feature of this area is a series of ice caves, small openings in the rocks along the base of the steep north slope of the mountain, out of which a continuous flow of cold air emerges in summer. Spring flowers, fall colors, or cool retreats welcome visitors to this small park.

Other maps: PA Highway map; PA Gazetteer, pg. 61; USGS topo, Alexandria, & Franklinville quads; Rothrock State Forest map; MSTA map #201.

Getting there: Take PA 26 south to Pine Grove Mills and continue on PA 45 west through Seven Stars and Franklinville. Look on the left for the entrance to the park, which is about 2 miles east of the village of Spruce Creek. When you reach Spruce Creek you have gone too far. Turn around and go back a mile or two and look again for that obscure entrance, on the right this time. There is a small historic marker sign and a bridge to cross at the entrance. Park in the parking area.

MAP FOR COLERAIN PARK

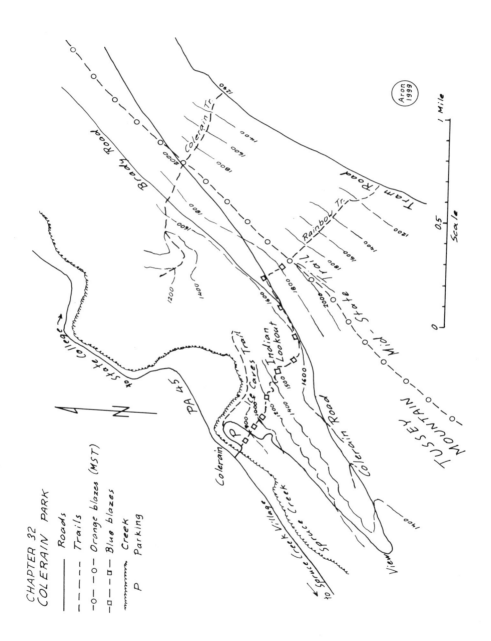

Hike description: Begin part one of your hike along the creek; follow the park road (Colerain Road) upstream. Soon you will see a well-worn but unblazed path on your left, continuing upstream close to the creek. Follow it for about half an hour. There are some very large hemlock trees to hug, and also ancient beech trees whose smooth bark holds an accumulation of carved initials. Although some people say the best way to recognize a beech tree is by the carvings on its trunk, it is doubtful that the tree enjoys wearing nametags.

Many flowers grow on the banks. In May look for the blossoms of sharp-lobed hepatica, fringed polygala, wild ginger and jack-in-the-pulpit. The ice caves are found along this trail. After you have hiked past three or four ice caves the trail ends. Return to the park the way you came. In the lawn you may notice the small purple-flowered gill-over-the-ground, a member of the mint family, once used instead of hops to flavor beer and ale.

Now that you are warmed up, you can begin the more serious part of the hike. Start walking up Colerain Road until you reach the crossing of the blue blazed trail which began near the parking area. Turn left off the road and follow the blazes up the old trail. The climb, through a series of switchbacks, is relentlessly up. Take your time. Look for trailing arbutus on the trail near the last 2 or 3 switchbacks. The view improves as you go up the mountain. A thick patch of redbud trees provides color in the valley in early May. Later, one can see dogwood dotting the hillsides with white.

Whenever we climb the trail at Colerain, it seems to get steeper every year. Some people will love it, and others will think I am trying to "do them in". I always remember a friend from India who used to regard this as her favorite hike. While most of us struggled, she, clad in simple sari and sandals, would seem to float, effortlessly and serenely to the top. All things are not equal to all people.

At 0.7 mile you reach Indian Lookout. The view from the rocky overlook provides a glimpse of the distant Allegheny Plateau. This is one of the more spectacular autumn color scenes. Stay back from the edge, behind the stone wall; the precipice is steep, and more dangerous than it looks. Lives have been lost here!

After a short rest and lunch at the overlook, continue on the blue-blazed trail, which emerges in 1/4 mile on Colerain Road. Turn right and follow this unpaved forestry road back down to the park. More dogwood trees and some wild azalea are found along this stretch. After a mile the road curves sharply to the right, showing a broad vista of farmland to the west. It then descends gently for another mile into Colerain Picnic Area. When you reach the blue blazes, turn left and follow them down to your car.

ODE TO ARBUTUS
(c) 1984 Jean Aron

A lowly, struggling wayside artist,
trodden down, again springs up
triumphant.

Attempting not to gain great heights,
But spreading to embrace the Earth,
She draws her subtle fragrance
from the sun.

Created from the rocks and sky,
A splash of beauty, quickly passing,
delicate.

Humbled here to childhood status,
Man the Mighty kneels before the blossom,
inhaling grace, as mother's milk,
from pink voluptuous bloom.

CHAPTER 33
LITTLE JUNIATA WATER GAP
Bridge to the Future

Summary: <u>4 miles, 2 hours</u>. Out and back walk along the river into the water gap natural area, on the proposed future route of Mid State Trail. See birds, wildflowers, rock cliffs, and the site of a hoped-for BIG footbridge. The more fit and fine hikers can also climb up the ridge on Mid State Trail for views of the gap from above. <u>1 mile up to the quarry level and 1 mile back; 2 hours</u>.

Location: 19 miles SW of State College. Start from PA 26 S.

Features: Water gaps, carved through mountain ridges by rivers, are common in the Appalachian ridge and valley province. Innately scenic, they are also convenient transportation routes. This is the only one in Pennsylvania which has no highway going through it. Once you have hiked back into the gap, out of earshot of traffic and train whistles, you can sink back into the quiet, and contemplate the geologic time it took to form this beautiful area.

History: Long used and appreciated by fishermen, birders, and naturalists, the Little Juniata Water Gap was recognized as a unique geologic and scenic area, and officially designated a Pennsylvania State Natural Area sometime in the 1970's.

The Mid State Trail was extended to the Natural Area around 1978, and soon after was continued , via the railroad bridge, across the river, and over Short Mountain to US 22. Problems with this route arose in 1994 and 1995, when a second track was placed on the Conrail bridge, and the tunnels were enlarged. It was no longer possible nor permitted to use the trail route. Hikers were forced to use an alternate way through the village of Barree.

MAP FOR LITTLE JUNIATA WATER GAP

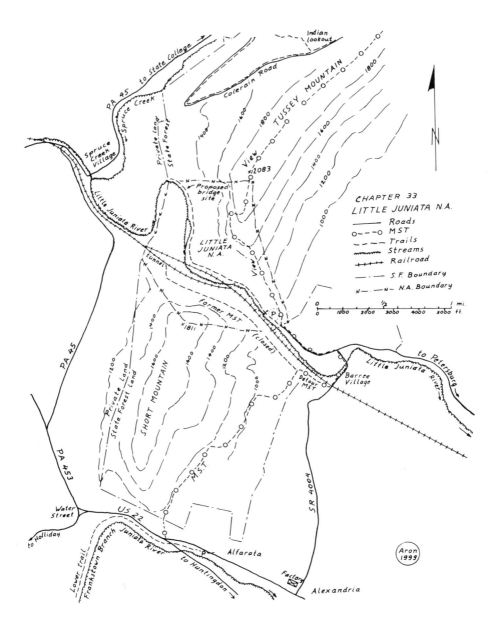

Since 1994 the Mid State Trail Association has pursued the idea of building a footbridge across the Little Juniata River. The span of 130 feet, would not be easy or cheap. A $70,000 factory-made bridge was proposed. State Forestry officials are in favor of the idea, but technical problems continue to surface. Still there is optimism that the bridge will become a reality by the end of year 2000. If and when the new bridge becomes a reality, the Mid State Trail will be relocated along the riverside, and the Natural Area will be a little more accessible on both sides of the river. MSTA (*a non-profit corporation*) has started a fund for the Little Juniata Bridge, and is accepting contributions. For more information, write to P.O. Box 167, Boalsburg, PA 16827. Or call 814-466-9260.

Other maps: MSTA map #201; USGS topo, Alexandria quad; Rothrock State Forest map; PA Highway map; PA Gazetteer, page 61. See also, *Outbound Journeys in PA* by Marcia Bonta, 1987.

Getting there: Start from West College Ave./ PA 26 South. Drive to Pine Grove Mills. Continue on PA 45 heading southwest through Spruce Creek to a junction with PA 453. Turn left; keep left at the junction with US 22, towards Huntingdon. Turn left again on the road to Alexandria. Just after the factory, turn left on SR4004, to the village of Barree; cross a bridge, turn left again on a road ending at the parking lot of Little Juniata Natural Area.

Hike description: If it is a fine day, and you want to hike up the mountain for the views, you should do it *first*. Caution: The relentless climb may be very tough for short hikers, so before you undertake such adventure, consider your fitness level and that of others in your party, as well as how clear the day is for vista gazing. The views may be magnificent on a really clear day, or nothing much in the fog or haze, but the mountain is consistently steep every day. Don't be ashamed to skip this challenging, but optional part of the trip. If you decide to try it, be prepared, carry drinking water, etc. You can opt to turn back at any time.

To climb the mountain for the views: Find the orange blazed trail to the right (east) of the parking lot, and follow it uphill. The vertical rise is about 900 feet over 1 mile. In half a mile you get the first view across the gap. A few hundred feet farther you reach the first quarry level, where Tuscarora sandstone (ganister) was taken a century ago. It was used mainly for lining in iron furnaces. In 1 mile you reach a view of Short Mountain across the water gap at 1600 ft. elevation. You can turn back here, or continue to climb up an old funicular grade, and in another 3/4 mile you will reach the very top of Tussey Ridge at 2000 ft. elevation, with one of the most extensive views in the state. On a clear day you can see over three folds of the ridge all the way to Blue Knob State Park

To do just the short hike into the gap: start hiking north from the parking lot on an old road; pass a gate and continue on the former Mid State Trail for 3/4 mile. The trail into the gap continues ahead with the river on your left. and the mountain on your right. Look for wildflowers: violets, Solomon's seal and jack-in-the-pulpit. A belted kingfisher may swoop across the water.

About halfway into the 1-mile gap, someone has outfitted an open grove with log and stone benches around a campfire ring. This pleasant spot is one of the few wider areas on the trail. Continue picking your way along the riverside trail. Notice the interesting rock outcroppings, and some tiny waterfalls entering from the right. Pass an island, where the river splits in two and then rejoins. When you reach a boundary with private land, you must turn around.

The site for the proposed footbridge is a few hundred feet before the boundary, at a place where the banks on both sides are relatively high, and the foundations can be anchored in the rock. Perhaps, if you are reading this in the 21st century, there is a real bridge already there. If not, try to imagine one. What a fine long hike you could make, if there were a bridge. Let us hope. For the present you must turn back and retrace your steps to your car.

CHAPTER 34
BALD EAGLE PARK
Short Walks Near a Long Lake

Summary: Two trails are available. 1)The Butterfly Trail and other mowed paths provide a gentle loop, 3 miles; 2 hours walking, on the north side of the lake, with nearby swimming, fishing, picnicking and modern campground. 2) The Lakeside Trail, 5.5 miles; 3 hours walking, on the south lake shore, is mostly level, and loops through a hardwood forest near the more remote primitive campground. Either trail could be x-c skied. In addition, 4 miles of x-c ski trails can be found on the north side of the highway.

Location: 21 miles NE of State College. Start from PA 26 N.

Features: Bald Eagle Valley is interesting topographically. It lies in a transition zone between the Appalachian Mountains and the Allegheny Plateau. Bald Eagle Ridge is the northernmost of a series of parallel Appalachian ridges which form the ridge and valley region. To the northwest, the Allegheny Plateau begins.

The lake is a BIG lake--1730 acres, 8 miles long, with 23 miles of shoreline. It lies in a big valley, in a big park--5900 acres. It can handle a big crowd. It is a place for big motorboats, water skiers; big cabin sailboats, or pontoon houseboats. It harbors big fish -- muskie, pickerel, and northern pike; big birds -- migrating waterfowl; a snowy egret; a bald eagle; as well as woodland birds, and meadow-loving birds, such as bluebirds, and a rare orchard oriole. There is space for all at the big-hearted park which bears the name of our national symbol.

History: Actually Bald Eagle State Park, as well as the mountain, valley and creek, were named for Indian Chief Bald Eagle of the Leni-Lenape, or Delaware, tribes who lived here before 1720.

MAP FOR BALD EAGLE PARK

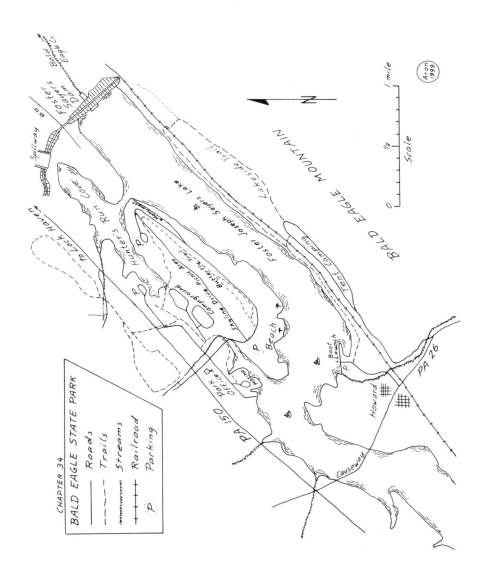

The Foster Joseph Sayers Dam, formerly Blanchard Dam, a flood control project built by the U.S. Army Corps of Engineers, was completed in 1969. It was named in memory of a Centre County man who was posthumously awarded the Congressional Medal of Honor for heroic service in WWII. The Pennsylvania Department of Environmental Resources assumed operating responsibilities in 1971 and the State Park was opened on the 4th of July that year.

Other maps: PA Highway; PA Gazetteer, pgs. 48 & 62; USGS topo, Howard quad; Bald Eagle S. F. map; Bald Eagle State Park.

Getting there: Follow PA 26 north. At the Y (Nittany Mall) keep left and follow PA 150 north through Bellefonte and Milesburg (14 miles). Cross a bridge over Bald Eagle Creek and at the big highway interchange (I-80) keep following PA 150 north about 10 miles. Notice the causeway which crosses the lake to the town of Howard on the south shore. You will cross here later. But on your first visit to the park, stay on PA 150 north another 1.5 miles and turn right to the Park Office for maps and information.

Hike description: 1) To hike the Butterfly Trail, proceed past the marina towards the beach. Park anywhere near the bathhouse, restrooms or picnic area. Locate the trail by looking towards the beach and to the left (east) until you see a large bulletin board and trail sign. The trail markers are hiker/ skier silhouettes on a brown background. Begin hiking on the mowed paths through open fields, where wildflowers are sown to encourage a variety of butterflies. Check the display board for information about butterflies.

The Butterfly Loop itself is 1.2 miles. You can go around it or just do one side of it, depending on the season and your interest. An attractive small pond lies in the middle of the loop. You can pass it on either side. Continue in a northeasterly direction, with the lake on your right, gradually climbing the hill, until you emerge on Skyline Drive, about halfway on your 3-mile hike.

Cross the road and continue following the hiker silhouette trail markers, now in the shade of the woods. The trail winds gradually downhill, with views over Hunter Run Cove.

After crossing the shallow west end of the cove on a boardwalk bridge, continue straight (north) on a shady path behind the campsites. After crossing a ditch find a mowed path again, turn left (west) parallel to the campground road. *For future reference: Near the campground you pass another mowed path, heading north up to the highway. This would connect with another 4-mile hiking/ skiing loop located north of PA 150.*

Look for the campground entrance kiosk, and find the mowed path behind it heading south and west back to the main park road near the marina. Follow the road to the left until you find your car.

2) The Lakeside Trail is a rougher, wilder hike than the Butterfly, and more remote, but with cool woodland shade. Some campers will readily forego the comforts of the modern campground for the quiet solitude and deep woods of the primitive south shore.

To hike Lakeside Trail, return south on PA 150. Turn left on PA 26 south and drive across the causeway and through Howard. Just before PA 26 crosses the overpass over the railroad tracks, turn left, drive 1/2 mile, and park at the Bald Eagle boat launch area.

The Lakeside Trail starts just behind the restrooms, beginning as a mowed path. As the name indicates, the trail follows the lake side. In 1 mile you reach a junction with a trail coming down from the Primitive Campground. Take note. You will be returning this way.

Stay on the left, close to the lake. Soon the trail becomes an apparent old road, continuing along the lakeside for another 1.5 miles. In spring you may find Jack-in-the-pulpit, violets and gill-over-the-ground. In July the tall white spikes of blossoms are black cohosh or bugbane. The ferns are mostly hay-scented ferns, called "thrice-cut ferns"--very frilly, and our most common fern. Can you see why these lacey plants are called thrice cut? Sometimes you may see deer tracks or even deer -- like the spotted twin fawns who greeted me one day. The colorless or white saprophytic flower, shaped like a pipe, is of course Indian pipe. As you get nearer the dam, the path is "paved" with large flat stones.

The trail emerges in a grassy open area near an underpass culvert. This is the halfway point. Your hike turns right here, through the tunnel, and up into the woods. Bear right, heading back west.

On the upper path look for hepatica, mayapples; partridge berry, wild grapes; and later blue-eyed grass. It is a more open woodland than the lower section; you can move more easily. Listen for the woodthrush trying to sing louder than the motorboat.

Another 1.5 miles through the woods brings you out onto the road at the east end of the campground loop. Turn right on the road and follow it a little way downhill until you find the trail going back down to the Lakeside. You may see a hiker sign and an arrow marking the trail. Follow it down through another culvert underpass beneath the railroad. At the junction you noted before, turn left and retrace the first mile of trail back to your car.

Note: Do NOT cross the railroad any place other than the culverts. It may be tempting to walk along the tracks, but that way is not fun, may be dangerous, and <u>will not take you to your car</u>.

On the return drive you may wish to turn left on PA 26 and follow it south and west through Pleasant Gap and all the way back to State College (25 miles). This way is a bit more "scenic", a euphemism for narrow and winding, but it is actually the shortest way, and is an interesting route in good weather.

CHAPTER 35
POE PADDY/ POE VALLEY
Sparkling Waters plus Penn's View

Summary: A variety of hiking possibilities are found in Bald Eagle State Forest and two State Parks.

#1)<u>Very short hikers</u> can pursue <u>gentle hikes on a 3-mile</u> section of Mid State Trail which runs along Penn's Creek on a railroad grade, across a footbridge and through a tunnel.

#2)The <u>moderately ambitious</u> short hikers can do a 2-car shuttle hike, <u>4 miles; 3 hours,</u> from Poe Paddy to Poe Valley State Park, using a former Mid State Trail route, over a hill and beside a brook.

#3)The <u>strongest hikers</u> can do the shuttle using the newer Mid State Trail route, <u>climbing to the top</u> of Long Mountain for the views; a slightly longer and more strenuous hike.

#4)The <u>truly intrepid hikers,</u> with only one car, can combine the second and third options into an <u>8 mile leg buster</u> all day outing.

Location: 25 miles east of State College. Start from US 322 E.

Features: There is something about free-flowing water which fascinates us. Perhaps it is the instinctive knowledge that water is life. Our bodies are 65% water. Watching water move gives us a feeling of freedom, as though we were moving with the same lithe grace and agility as the brook. This area has water in many forms, from Penn's Creek and Big and Little Poe Creeks to the lake at Poe Valley. No matter which hike you choose, you are sure to enjoy the water. Camping, fishing and swimming are also available.

History: Poe Paddy State Park began as the overflow campground for Poe Valley, but it has attractions of its own. In 1880 it was the site of Poe Mills, a lumbering camp with a population of 400. Situated at the confluence of Penn's Creek and Big Poe Creek, it is a favorite with fishermen. Many hiking trails pass through or nearby, including the Mid State Trail.

Other maps: USGS topo, Coburn quad; Bald Eagle State Forest map; Mid State Trail Map #205; Poe Valley State Park map.

Getting there: Follow US 322 east through Boalsburg and Potter's Mills. From the 4-lane divided highway in the Seven Mountains area, about 15 miles from State College, turn left (east) onto Sand Mountain Road. Signs guide you to Poe Valley State Park, via 9 miles of gravel roads. There are many other ways to get to the park, but this is the easiest.

In Big Poe Valley you reach a stretch of paved road with private homesites. Beyond these, still on the paved road, is the entrance to Poe Valley State Park. Turn off into the Park and stop at the park office for maps and information. Proceed to the upper tier of the parking lot. If you are doing the shuttle hike, #2 or #3, park a car near the blue-blazed Hunter's Path, your end point. Poe Valley Park contains a small lake for non-motorized boating and fishing, swimming, picnicking and camping. Restrooms, drinking water and telephone are available, making it a pleasant place for hikers to wait after the hike while drivers shuttle cars.

Drive around the one-way parking loop past the beach, and back to the main road (Big Poe Valley Road). Turn right (east) and reach Poe Paddy State Park in 3.5 miles. Turn left into this Park and station your car in Big Poe Creek parking lot near the bridge.

Hike description: #1) Many gentler hikes are possible from Poe Paddy. Fishermen's paths on either side of Penn's Creek let you walk upstream or downstream short distances along the bank, through hemlock, rhododendron and jack-in-the-pulpit. 0.6 mile east on the dead end road (orange-blazed MST), the old railroad bridge, which is now a footbridge, is the only way across Penn's Creek for miles around.

MAP FOR POE PADDY

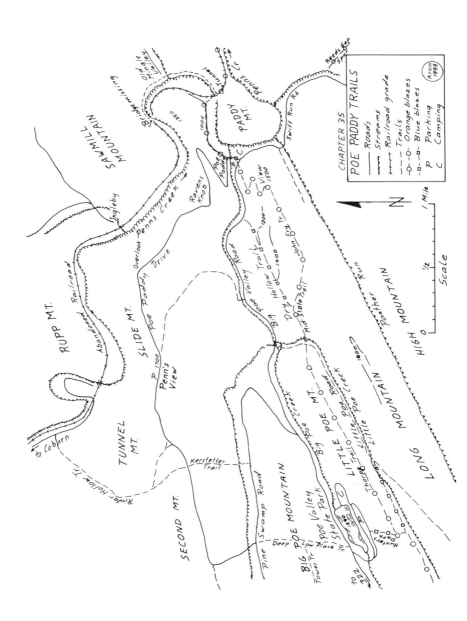

It is interesting to walk through the tunnel, which is just beyond the bridge. Penn's Creek formed S-curves around the rocky peninsula, but the railroad tunneled through it. Beyond the tunnel the easy cinder path follows the left bank of Penn's Creek on a 3-mile rail trail. This is the ONLY piece of Mid State Trail suitable for bicycles.

Hike description, shuttle hikes: The orange-blazed Mid State Trail connecting Poe Paddy to Poe Valley Park was re-routed in 1980/81. One new section follows the top of Little Poe Mountain; another is high on Long Mountain. The more energetic hiker may enjoy this newer route, shuttle hike #3. It begins just opposite the entrance to Poe Paddy State Park on the John E. Fry Trail, named for a local man who was a diligent overseer for this section of Mid State Trail. A challenging climb up switchbacks takes you to vistas, interesting rock slabs, (watch out for rattlers), and a chance to look down on soaring hawks. But this route is more difficult, longer, and away from the sparkling water of Little Poe Creek.

The short hiker might choose the older Mid State Trail route, shuttle hike #2 . From Poe Paddy walk back (west) 1/2 mile on Big Poe Valley Road (the one you came on). Look for the blue-blazed Dry Hollow Trail on the left. Follow Dry Hollow Trail heading southwest gradually uphill 3/4 mile. The underbrush -- huckleberry, mountain laurel, ferns, etc.-- is thriving and is quick to overgrow the trail, but the footway is well-worn. Listen to the calls of the rufous-sided towhee, advising you to "drink your tea-hee-hee", or perhaps you'll hear the fluting call of a woodthrush. Follow the blue blazes until you reach a trail register at an intersection. *Here the Mid State Trail to the left (east) goes back to Poe Paddy via the top of Long Mountain (the newer route). This could make a 3-mile circuit hike, if you don't have a second car.* But the shuttle hike to Poe Valley continues straight ahead (west) on the orange blazes, a quarter mile down a dry hollow to Little Poe Creek.

There is space beside the creek to pause in this cool, shady retreat, to hear the rushing lullaby of the water, eat lunch, and poke around the small pond in springtime to find frogs' eggs.

Cross Little Poe Creek on a bridge built by Keystone Trails Association's TrailCare Team on May 5, 1991. Across Little Poe Road, another ambitious new section of MST climbs steeply up Little Poe Mountain on stone steps. This is the Thorpe Trail, named for Richard Thorpe a former State Forester. The "big kids" on the #3 shuttle hike might go on this newer route, but #2 hikers want to stay near the water, so you turn left on the road instead.

Little Poe Road is gated and not maintained, so there is no traffic. It is an easy mile as you stroll upstream along the clear, bubbling brook with a thousand crystal waterfalls tumbling through spillways of moss-covered stones.

About 0.2 mile after the road crosses to the other side of the brook, look for the blue-blazed Little Poe Trail on the right. Cross the stream again on stepping stones and continue on blue 1/2 mile upstream on a good trail until you reach orange again at Hunter's Path. Turn right and climb up the south side of Little Poe Mountain. It is very steep, but only 0.1 mile.

On top, the orange MST heads east along this ridge on the Thorpe Trail. If the "big kids" on the #3 shuttle have taken this trail they may be here already. The intrepid #4 hikers can head back from here on whichever orange or blue path was not taken on the way out -- doing an 8-mile figure eight.

The Hunter's Path is blue-blazed going down the north side 1/4 mile to your shuttle car at Poe Valley Lake.

Bonus: PENN'S VIEW, Autumn Destination

If time permits take a drive to one of the best views in Pennsylvania, just two air miles (5 road miles) north of Poe Valley. Located in Penn Township, this glorious scene of wooded hills, valleys and streams, which looks out across Penn's Creek and Penn's Valley would have to be called Penn's View. It is doubtful whether founder William Penn ever saw it, but I'm sure he would have liked it.

You could hike to Penn's View using a variety of trails and dirt roads, or you can drive. From Poe Valley State Park, drive one mile east, turn left on Pine Swamp Road, a rough rocky road which climbs up Big Poe Mountain. In two miles turn right on the somewhat smoother Poe Paddy Drive and find Penn's View in another two miles.

Or, from Poe Paddy State Park, drive up Poe Paddy Drive, a total of 3 miles, pausing for views at Raven's Knob and Ingleby Overlook, which looks down at the village of Ingleby and across to Elk Gap and Sawmill Mountain.

From Penn's View the distant scenery includes the gap between Brush Mountain and Shriner Mountain, with Nittany Mountain beyond them. To the right of the scene, smaller Rupp Mountain rises beside Penn's Creek. The Penn's View vista looks north over an S-curve of Penn's Creek near the village of Coburn. Tunnel Mountain and a railroad footbridge are visible below. This is the same railroad grade that goes through Poe Paddy, with a similar bridge and tunnel. You can hike from Coburn tunnel to Poe Paddy, about 4 miles along the grade; but the last mile is a bit rugged because a bridge is missing, so the hiker has to follow newly forged trails on the rocky left bank.

To return a different way: From Penn's View drive west on Poe Paddy Drive 1.9 miles. Turn right onto Pine Swamp Road and follow it out 2.2 miles to Siglerville/ Millheim Pike. Turn right (north), enjoy a vista in 0.2 mile, and then drive down 2.5 miles more to Penn's Creek, a total of 6.8 miles from Penn's View to the paving.

Across the bridge a paved road SR 2012 follows the creek. If you want to visit Coburn and the other tunnel, turn right. In Coburn turn sharp right, cross a bridge and then turn left, following the road along the right bank of Penn's Creek. Park near the big bend where the railroad tunnel goes through Tunnel Mountain, or drive around and park on the other end of the tunnel.

If you're not going to Coburn, turn left on the paved SR 2012, which follows the creek through rural scenery 6 miles to Spring Mills. Turn left on PA 45 to return to Boalsburg and State College.

CHAPTER 36
THOUSAND STEPS
Stairway to History

Summary: 4.5 miles, 3 hours, up and down. Warm up hike of 1.5 miles on the more level "dinkey" trail, before tackling the steep 0.75 mile of stone steps, rising 800 feet to the top of Jack's Mountain in Huntingdon County. Return the same way.

Features: The stone steps were placed in 1936, by quarry workers, who used them as a quick route to their work. Many old narrow gauge railroad beds are still visible along the contour lines on the mountain. There is a "dinkey" repair shed near the top, where the steam engines were overhauled. There are many fine views from different levels, overlooking Jack's Narrows.

History: From the 1930's until 1952 the silica-rich sandstone, called ganister, was quarried by Harbison Walker Refractories Company. Workers would climb the steps every day, 1000 feet up Jack's Mountain, to get to their jobs at the quarry, loading the heavy rocks into railroad cars. The dinkey steam engines then pulled the cars on zig-zag tracks down the mountain to a factory in Mount Union. The stone was crushed and formed into silica bricks. These yellow, heat resistant bricks were used to line the furnaces which produced steel, iron, and glass. The half-million bricks a day produced in Mount Union made it the "Silica Brick Capital of the World". By 1985 changes in steel production reduced demand for silica bricks, and Harbison-Walker closed their plant.

A proposal for the Link Trail, to "link" Mid State Trail System at Greenwood Furnace S.P. with Tuscarora Trail at Cowans Gap S.P., was begun by Keystone Trails Association in 1980. A route for the 70-mile trail was explored by Dave Raphael, Tom Thwaites, Ron Shafer and others. But it was Bob Olsen, a retired Penn State Professor, who took on the big job of getting the trail constructed.

MAP FOR THOUSAND STEPS

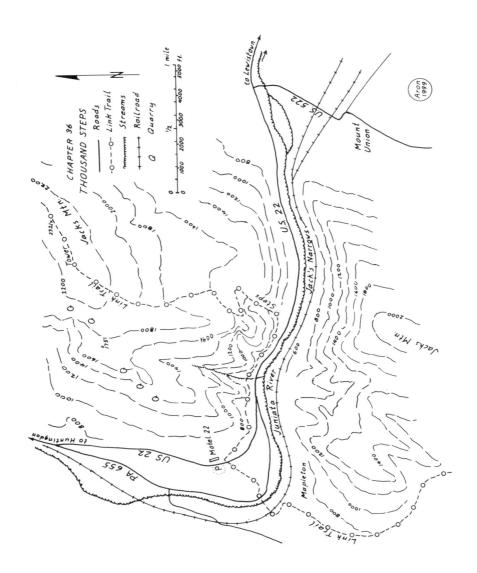

In 1981 Bob Olsen began working with volunteers and state agencies to build the Link Trail. He organized overseers to maintain it. By 1985 the Trail was blazed and ready, and a set of maps and guide was printed. Harbison-Walker granted KTA an easement for the Link Trail to traverse the "Thousand Steps".

Despite the efforts of the 1980's, the ravages of gypsy moths and subsequent low usage began to take its toll. The Link Trail was looking a little ragged. Then in the early 1990's another intrepid trail worker stepped forward. Mike Sausser, from Schuylkill Haven, PA, took on the job of revitalizing the Link Trail once more. Sausser brought an energy to the coordinator's job which reactivated people. By 1997 the Trail was once more passable.

Then in 1997 Harbison-Walker decided to sell the 669 acres containing the Thousand Steps. In order to secure the Link Trail and protect the Steps and their surroundings for public recreational and historical values, a coalition of groups headed by KTA, the Mount Union Area Historical Society, and Central Pennsylvania Conservancy (CPC), came together to purchase the tract, with help from DCNR and Western PA Conservancy. On October 30, 1998 the tract was officially deeded to CPC. Ultimately the property will be turned over to the Game Commission, except for the Link Trail right of way and the "dinkey house" area. Of the $190,000 purchase price, half came from a DCNR state grant; the rest was contributed by groups and individuals. Contributors could "purchase" one or more of the Thousand Steps at $100 each, with certain prime steps going for $500 or $1000 each. *Some steps may still be available. For information write to Mount Union Area Historical Society, P.O. Box 1776, Mount Union, PA 17066.*
For further explorations on Link Trail, order a guide and maps from KTA, P.O. Box 251, Cogan Station, PA 17728.

Other maps: USGS topo, Mount Union quad; Rothrock S. F. map; KTA Link Trail guide & maps; *"PA Hiking Trails"*, 1998.

Location: 28 miles south of State College. Start from PA 26 S.

Getting there: Follow PA 26 south through Huntingdon. Turn east on US 22, drive another 7 miles. Look for parking on the right hand side of the road, opposite Motel 22. *If you want to skip the 1.5 mile warmup trail, and go directly to the Steps, some limited parking may be found along the north side of the highway at Jacks Springs, located 1 mile farther east. A short, blue-blazed trail, just east of the spring, goes directly up to the base of the Steps.*

Hike description: Cross the highway with great care. Look to the right (east) for a trail sign and orange blazes. Begin walking eastward, on a level grade about 200 feet above the highway.

In half a mile, as you cross the first of three ravines, look up high to the west to see an interesting rock formation called "Hags Rump". You may also pass a lookout point called "Lizard's View"

In 1.5 miles you reach the foot of Thousand Steps. *A blue trail to the right descends to US 22 at Jacks Spring.* Turn left and begin climbing the steps. Stop often to check the views, drink water, and smile. Remember the workers who climbed these steps daily could do it in 30 minutes. Give yourself at least one hour.

Near the top, the trail levels off and goes past "the dinkey shed". If you are nimble enough to climb onto the roof, there are nice views to be had. One day, a plaque may be installed, displaying the names of all groups and persons who "purchased" a step.

You can turn around after the dinkey shed, or continue another 15 minutes or so, up a few more steps for some more good views.

Coming down the steps should take about half as long as going up, but you still have to watch your step -- literally. You can also watch mine and everyone else's, even your own if you buy one.

CHAPTER 37
LOWER TRAIL
Flower of Rail Trails

Summary: <u>5-mile super easy stroll</u> along a shaded stream corridor -- the northern half of an 11-mile rail trail along the Frankstown Branch of the Juniata River. The trail is owned and managed by Rails-To-Trails of Central Pennsylania, Inc., P.O. Box 592, Hollidaysburg, PA 16648. For information, call 814-832-2400.

Location: 26 miles SW of State College. Start from PA 26 S.

Features: On a shuttle hike from Mt. Etna to Alfarata, history, wildflowers, and birds will pique your interest. You can hike, bicycle, or horseback ride along this very smooth level walkway. Comfortable walking shoes are adequate. You will want to come back soon and do the other half, starting from Williamsburg.

History: The Frankstown Branch of the Juniata River has always been an important transportation corridor. Early American Indians traveled along it as the Kittanning Trail. Pioneering settlers knew it as the Frankstown Road. In 1832 the Juniata Division of the Pennsylvania Canal, from Duncannon to Hollidaysburg was opened on this river as part of the Main Line "continuous waterway", which linked Philadelphia and Pittsburgh. Then came the railroads, which by the 1880's had taken over most of the traffic. The Petersburg Branch of the Pennsylvania Railroad (PRR) was active until 1979, and was formally abandoned in 1982. Now it is your turn to tread this path of history.

In 1991 a generous donation by T. Dean Lower made it possible for Rails-to-Trails to purchase this 11 mile section. The trail is named in memory of his wife, Jane Y. and son Roger D. Lower. Another 3.5 miles of trail were acquired in 1999. Future plans are to extend Lower Trail 6.5 miles, into Canoe Creek State Park.

MAP FOR LOWER TRAIL

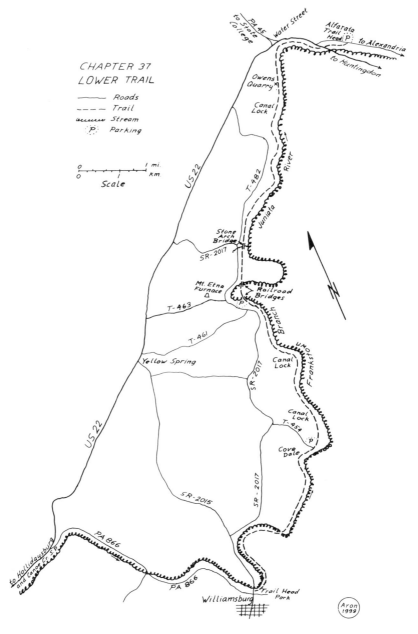

Other maps: USGS topo, Spruce Creek, & Williamsburg quads; MSTA map #218; Lower Trail map by RTT of Central PA; PA Gazetteer, pages 61 & 75. See also, *PA Hiking Trails* by KTA 1998; and *Pennsylvania's Great Rail-Trails* by Rails-to-Trails Conservancy, PA Chapter.

Getting there: Follow PA 26 south to Pine Grove Mills and then PA 45 southwest through Spruce Creek. At the T intersection with Route 453 turn left and drive 0.7 mile to a Y intersection with US 22. Keep left on US 22 East toward Huntingdon. In another half mile, turn left onto the first road to Alexandria. After a railroad grade crossing, at 0.4 mile from US 22, turn sharp right into the parking lot of the Alfarata trailhead, opened in 1994.

After leaving a car here, at the end point of your hike, go back on US 22, turn left (west) toward Hollidaysburg, and drive 4.9 miles. At a historic marker sign for Mt. Etna, turn left onto township road T-463. *Note: If you miss T-463, then try T-461 which leaves U.S. 22 in another 0.6 mile, just before Yellow Spring. Both roads go to the Mt. Etna area, but T-463 is more interesting.* Drive gently through this rustic farm area. A bucolic mile on T-463 will get you to Mt. Etna Iron Furnace and village

Built in 1809 and operated until 1877, Mt. Etna Furnace produced some of the Juniata iron for which this region was famous. It was the best iron in America until the rise of coal and coke iron making. Many of the historic sites and buildings are still standing, such as the ironworkers' bunkhouse. At 1.2 miles along this road you pass the partially restored furnace stack. In another 0.2 mile you reach the riverside road SR-2017. Turn right and drive 0.4 mile passing three primitive log houses. Just before reaching the large, fancy but now decrepit, ironmaster's mansion, near the junction with T-461, turn left into the trailhead parking lot. A picnic shelter and a portable restroom are available at this midway point of the Trail.

Hike description: Begin hiking the trail to the left heading north. The river makes an oxbow bend at Mt. Etna. The railroad did not bother to fit into all those curves. Instead, two large bridges were built, to keep its lines straight. Rails-to-Trails reconstructed them with all new decking in 1993/94. Excellent workmanship of both the past and the present is seen in these nearly 200 ft. long bridges.

The next stop is the Stone Arch Bridge over Fox Run on the Huntingdon/ Blair County line. As you approach look for a large mill pond on the left, graced by weeping willows, and a red barn often reflected in its waters. Just past the pond, opposite the red barn, the trail crosses the Stone Arch Bridge. It was once an aqueduct of the canal, plus both a road and a stream passed beneath it -- a real traffic hub. Come down the side trail off the bridge for a brief look at it from below. It has a proverbial keystone in its arch.

As you continue on the trail watch for birds and wildflowers. Listen for colorful songsters such as the scarlet tanager, northern oriole, Carolina wren, red-eyed vireo, wood thrush. Look for red trilliums, Dutchman's-breeches, and yellow corydalis. In summer, you may find hairy beard tongue and panicled hawkweed. You will pass more historic sites: Canal Lock No. 53 and Goodman Quarry; Canal Channel.; and a trail register near Owens Quarry, the last marked site before arriving back at Alfarata.

After picking up the shuttle car from Mt. Etna, you can opt to drive home a different way. You came following the north side of Tussey Ridge, passing through the gap at Water Street. The return follows the south side of Tussey Ridge, climbing over the mountain on PA 26 -- just two miles longer, and quite scenic. From Mt. Etna take T-461, 2 miles back to US 22. Turn right and drive back through Alexandria. Follow PA 305 through Petersburg to Mooresville. Go straight, passing the Stone Valley Recreation Area to PA 26. Turn left to State College. The total return driving distance this way is 35.4 miles.

CHAPTER 38
CANOE CREEK PARK
Lime Kilns and Nature

Summary: <u>4 miles; 3 hours,</u> moderately easy; Moore's Hill Trail in a State Park in Blair County features a variety of birds and wildflowers in a mixed hardwood forest, near streams and marshes.

Location: 33 miles SW of State College. Start from PA 26 S.

Features: On a hot, summer day, start in the cool of morning and plan for a swim at the park beach afterwards. Or, late risers could do the trip on a summer's evening. The park is open year-round, and winter activities include x-c skiing, ice skating, and sledding. Fall color is beautiful here, as in most Pennsylvania mixed forests. But we think the best season for Canoe Creek is spring. The abundance of yellow lady slippers around the first week in May, combined with the bonus of many other wildflowers throughout the season, has put Canoe Creek on our list of "must visit" places.

History: Ruins of lime kilns and limestone quarries offer historic interest. One of our newer state parks, dedicated in 1979, the 958-acre park holds a 155-acre recreation lake.

Other maps: USGS topo, Frankstown quad; Canoe Creek State Park map; PA Gazetteer, page 75; PA Highway map.

Getting there: The park is 12 miles east of Altoona, 1/2 mile off US 22 at the village of Canoe Creek. Follow directions in previous chapter to Lower Trail, but continue on US 22 another 5 miles west beyond the Mt. Etna turnoff. Follow signs. Pick up a map at the park office. Proceed to the beach area and park at the east end of the lot.

MAP FOR CANOE CREEK

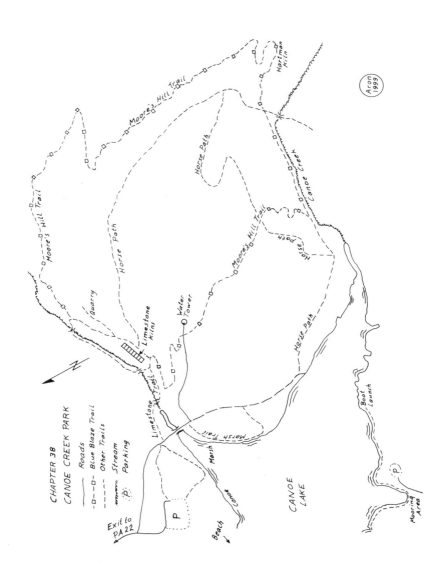

Hike description: Begin walking northeastward towards the Visitor Center or closer to the lake on Limestone Trail. Cross a paved park maintenance road. Continue on Limestone Trail to the historic site of the Blair County Limestone Company lime kilns. From 1900 to 1910 when these kilns operated, Pennsylvania led the nation in lime production. Lime was used in farming; in making iron and steel; in construction for mortar, plaster, and cement; in medicine; in purification of water; in soap, sugar, rubber, leather, ceramics, paint and more. Plan to spend a few minutes absorbing some of the fascinating information provided on historic markers.

If your time or your walking abilities are very limited, you could turn back after seeing the lime kilns; or complete just the 1-mile Limestone Trail, a relatively level path up one side of Mary Ann's Creek and back down the other. On a good day in birding and flowering season you won't know whether to look up or down. The short path alone can be a full day's outing for an avid birder.

To go the easiest route, with maximum flowers, turn left just before the kilns, cross a footbridge and follow the path along the right bank of Mary Ann's Run. Continue on Moore's Hill Trail to see the yellow lady slippers. When the path becomes too steep, you can turn around and go back the way you came.

For a longer, more strenuous hike, take the path up behind the kilns. Ignore for now the Moore's Hill Trail going steeply up the hill on the right. Your 4-mile loop will return you to that spot later. Also ignore the marked horse paths; just follow the hiking trail.

On an optional side-trip up to the quarry, you may find fossils in the rocks, orange flowers of butterfly-weed, or pink flowers of tick-trefoil, and rest on a bench at the north vista.

Caves in the quarry area are protected hibernation sites of Indiana bats, a U.S. endangered species. According to Joseph F. Merritt in Guide to Mammals of Pennsylvania (1987): "At one time, a total of about 5000 *M. sodalis* individuals were estimated to live in Pennsylvania. A recent population survey of all known cave sites for *Myotis sodalis* in Pennsylvania revealed, however, that only 150 individuals can still be found in the commonwealth."

Indiana bats are endangered because of human activities and disturbances during hibernation. Known sites are barricaded and posted against human intrusion. You will not see the bats nor the sites, but it is interesting and comforting to know they still exist. If you would like to know more, ask the park naturalist about evening walks or programs about bat biology. Find out how many mosquitoes each bat will eat.

From the quarry retrace your steps towards the kilns and turn sharp right downhill. In about 200 yards you reach a signed junction with Moore's Hill Trail. If you are doing just the 1-mile trip, turn left, cross a footbridge and head downstream.

For the 4-mile hike, turn right and follow the 3-inch triangle blue paint blazes, heading upstream. You would expect to find limestone-loving plants in this valley, and you do: bloodroot, hepatica, wild ginger, miterwort, and yellow lady slippers.

Soon the blazes veer to the right uphill, climbing steadily through two switchbacks. The trail is narrow and relentlessly upward, but only to the top. A red-eyed vireo sings. Bunchflowers and the white fairy candles of black cohosh line the path. The total rise is about 200 feet, as the trail skirts the north side of the hill and joins an old quarry road; elevation 1200 feet.

The trail descends through a woods of scrubby hawthorn, honeysuckle and redbud, on the east side of Moore's Hill.

Abundant poison ivy means long pants are preferable through this part. Recent trail work has greatly reduced this annoyance, but you should be alert. After passing another old concrete ruin, Hartman Kilns, continue southward on an old railroad bed in the Canoe Creek valley. Orange day lilies and yellow black-eyed Susans bloom in summer.

A pretty spot for lunch break is at the footbridge over Canoe Creek, which is on a side trail from Beaver Dam Road. The bridge is visible just before your trail makes a turn to the right. You might see bluebirds or tree swallows. Several dead trees with natural cavities are valuable nesting sites. The park also provides a number of bluebird boxes for these tenants.

Continue following the blue triangles downstream, along the right bank of Canoe Creek, towards the lake and the park. Look for a red Canada lily.

There is one more choice. Before reaching the lake, Moore's Hill Trail turns right and climbs over the south shoulder of the hill. If you cannot face another uphill, you can reach the park by staying on the trail closest to the water. Birders may see a bit more near the lake. Both a northern oriole and an orchard oriole were spotted there. However, it is a horse trail, and it can be muddy, and the lower trails are mostly in open sunny fields. If the day is hot, it may be better to stay in the shady woods on the hill. The choice is yours.

If you follow the blue triangles to the right, up some steps and a steep but short hill, squawroot and trillium are seen on the way. Several vistas give you an overview of the lake and surrounding mountains. Moore's Hill Trail ends at the kiln site where your loop began. Turn left and retrace your steps to your car. The swimming beach is open 11 AM to 7 PM Memorial Day to Labor Day. Restrooms and picnic shelters are a welcome convenience.

CHAPTER 39
PRINCE GALLITZIN
Forgotten Treasure

Summary: <u>4 miles, 2 hours</u>. Hike Crooked Run and Point Trails in a state park, on varied terrain, through a nature area, along a stream and near one small corner of the very large Lake Glendale. Add a visit to Headache Hill observation tower for an overview.

Location: 40 miles WSW of State College. Start from US 322 W.

Features: Situated on the Allegheny Plateau at an elevation of 1427 feet above sea level, the park land was acquired in 1957 with oil and gas lease funds, and was opened to recreation in 1965. In the first years, Prince Gallitzin State Park was thought of mostly as a sailing lake. The land was open and fairly treeless, and the wind was sometimes fickle, but interesting. Many people of the older generation may still remember it that way. News flash: trees grow a whole lot in 35 years. The park is very different and much improved. It is time to try it again.

Nature abounds in the 6,249-acre state park which contains a 1600-acre lake. Most activities center around the water. It is popular for sailboats and pontoon boats. You will find boating (up to 10 horsepower), fishing (warm water species) and swimming (beaches), as well as camping, winter sports, horseback riding, and some very nice, easy hiking trails. Gallitzin is a family destination. Located in Cambria County, north of Altoona, the drive from State College takes about an hour and a half.

Don't let the size of the park fool you. On any given day there may be hundreds of people enjoying various aspects, but you may not encounter anyone. Because Lake Glendale is a complex shape, divided into two main arms and many smaller bays and inlets, it is easy to find quiet corners. Most of the 26 miles of shoreline are

page 187

thickly wooded. Numerous deer, some of them almost tame, may be seen. Interesting birds can be spotted, especially around the wetland boardwalks. There is a lot to explore.

History: The park is named for Demetrius Augustine Gallitzin, a Catholic priest who established a frontier parish, the church of Saint Michael's, in 1799, and laid out the town of Loretto. Gallitzin had been born a Russian Prince, but in becoming a missionary priest he gave up his rights to nobility. He remained with his parish to his death in 1840.

Other maps: PA Highway map; PA Gazetteer, page 60; USGS topo, Coalport quad; Prince Gallitzin State Park map.

Getting there: Follow US 322 West to US 220/ I 99. Turn off and go through Tyrone northwest on PA 453. Turn left, southwest on PA 253 to PA 53 south, and follow the brown park signs. Your turnoff to the right is in the village of Frugality on SR 1026. Drive west about 2.5 miles and make a stop at the park office to pick up a map. You may also want to visit the nature center, which is at the main marina -- the turnoff just before the park office. Then continue driving around to the west side of the lake. Follow SR1026 for 2 more miles, then right on SR 1025 a short distance, then right on SR1021 for 2 miles. Look for the Crooked Run Nature Area. Park in the small parking lot on the left.

Hike description: About 1 mile of self-guided nature trail loops are found on the west side of the road. Do these first as a warm up. Follow the Footprint, Forest, and Deer Trails which make pleasant small loops through moist green woods (small green circles).

MAP FOR PRINCE GALLITZIN

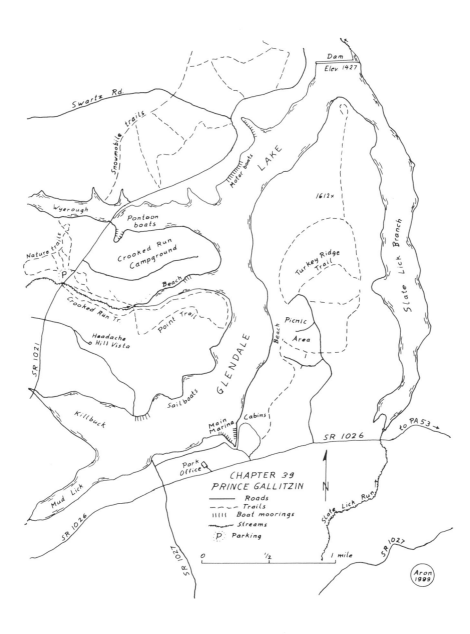

Then find Crooked Run Trail heading south across the run and across the road. It parallels the stream for 3/4 mile to a junction with Point Trail. Crooked Run and Point Trails form a sort of figure 8. They cross at the marshy west end of a small unnamed inlet. The swimming beach and boat launch of Crooked Creek Run Campground are on the north shore of this inlet. A boardwalk and platform near the marsh offer a resting and viewing spot for birders.

The Point Trail continues along the south shore of the inlet, with wildlife and wildflowers ready to surprise you. The trail bends south along the main lake. Half a mile away across the lake you can glimpse the Turkey Ridge beach area and picnic pavilions.

Point Trail begins to climb gradually uphill as it swings south and then turns abruptly back west on the return leg through more mature forest. Turn right at a trail junction and hike back down to the "figure 8" cross point at the marsh.

The last leg of your hike can be on the north side of the stream, or back the way you came. On the north side you pass through another small green circle called "Poems Trail", presumably inspired by the "Trees", as in Joyce Kilmer's poem.

Cross the road and find your car in Crooked Run Nature Trail lot. This hike is just one of many treasures to be found in this forgotten park. Many other possibilities invite you to come back soon.

On your way home, don't miss a visit to Headache Hill. Half a mile back from your hiking area, turn left (east). Follow signs to the hilltop. There is a large water tank for the park. Walk up the metal walkway to the top which forms a viewing platform. You can see most of the complex lake, and the dam, and the form of the peninsula where you hiked. A very satisfying finish to a full day.

CHAPTER 40
R. B. WINTER PARK
Also Good in Summer

Summary: Nature Trail, 1 mile loop; plus Lookout and Boiling Springs Trails, 2 miles. Total 3 miles in 2 hours. Other nearby hikes utilize the orange-blazed Mid State Trail and blue-blazed trails on Shriner Mountain cleared by the Penn State Outing Club.

Location: 40 miles ENE of State College. Start from US 322 E.

Features: A small and friendly place, R.B. Winter State Park is accessible and beautiful in all seasons of the year. The park lies cozily in a narrow valley 1500 feet above sea level. Trout fishing, hiking, swimming and camping; colorful autumns; ice-skating and x-c skiing lure many visitors to this scenic spot.

History: Formerly called Halfway Dam, the park and the earlier Halfway House tavern was at the halfway point through Brush Valley on the Fourteenmile Narrows Road. The road was used to transport farm produce by horse drawn wagon from Centre County to the Susquehanna River and the barge canal system. The present dam, which combines the waters of Rapid Run and Halfway Run into a 7-acre lake, was built by the Civilian Conservation Corps in 1933 to replace an old sawmill dam. It was the first stone masonry dam built by the CCC in the United States.

In 1955 the park was renamed R.B. Winter State Park in honor of Raymond B. Winter, a forester who spent 45 years working in this park and surrounding State Forest.

Other maps: USGS topo, Hartleton quad; Bald Eagle State Forest map; R.B. Winter State Park map; MSTA map #207; PSOC map #156/ Shriner Mtn. Trails. See also *PA Hiking Trails* by KTA.

Longer hikes: Follow the <u>9.1 mile</u> Halfway Cross Country Ski Trail, starting at a parking area east of the lake, using Bake Oven, Buffalo Flat, and Old Tram Trails to McCall Dam Road; then down the road and back along Rapid Run Nature Trail.

An <u>8-mile</u> hike up to Sand Mountain Tower is described in *50 Hikes in Central PA* by Tom Thwaites, 3rd edition - 1995.

A popular <u>20-mile</u> weekend backpack trip follows Mid State Trail between R.B. Winter State Park and Ravensburg State Park.

Getting there: The park is 18 miles west of Lewisburg, on PA 192. Take US 322 east to Boalsburg; follow PA 45 east to the traffic light at Old Fort; turn left on PA 144 and go 1 mile into Centre Hall; turn right on PA 192 and follow it 29 miles east to the park. Stop for maps and information at the park office on the right; then proceed another 0.1 mile to the picnic and beach parking lot, on the left just before you reach the lake and dam.

Hike description: Walk across the footbridge at the west end of the lake near the beach. At a sign for Rapid Run Nature Trail, turn left and soon left again on a straight wood chip path under the poleline. Rapid Run Trail is blazed with white dots. Walking shoes are adequate for this gentle trail which follows Rapid Run upstream, across a footbridge, and through cool hemlock woods. Rhododendron blooms in July, and Jack-in-the-pulpit and Indian pipe can be found. A solitary vireo sings. You are in cool open woods with about 90% hemlock trees. In 1/2 mile you cross Rapid Run again on a stone arch bridge, which was built in 1911 for the county road, now PA 192. The new highway and modern bridge are nearby for comparison. Follow white blazes north and then turn east on the return leg of the Rapid Run Trail.

The roof of the old Nature Center did not survive the winter of 1994. A bigger, better Environmental Center was built closer to the center of the park, north of the lake. The mounted wildlife displays make the new center worth a visit.

MAP FOR R.B. WINTER

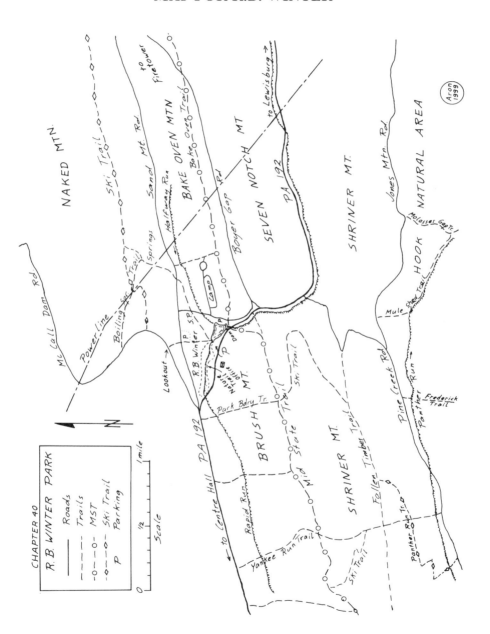

As you follow the white-dot-blazed northern leg of Rapid Run Nature Trail, you'll find some rhododendron, mosses, watercress, oxalis, and a few white pine trees. But the all-pervasive presence is still hemlock. The trees tower above you, fall beside you and spring up at your feet. You are walking on a carpet of tiny hemlock cones and thousands of hemlock seedlings.

After the second half mile you reach the signed Lookout Trail. Very short hikers can turn right here and follow the white dots back to the car, or the beach or dam, or the Environmental Center.

Most hikers will want to make the short climb to the overlook. Turn left on Lookout Trail and follow the red paint blazes. It is 1/3 mile up to the overlook, which is near McCall Dam Road. The trail does not become really steep until the last 600 feet, after crossing Sand Mountain Road. This trail has been rebuilt since 1994, with a gentler grade on easier switchbacks. The top, at elevation 1839 feet, is reached in about 15 minutes. The vista looks south over the lake and park. Rapid Run escapes through the gap into the Fourteen Mile Narrows. On the right are Brush Mountain, with taller Shriner Mountain behind it; while Bake Oven Mountain and Seven Notch Mountain are visible on the left.

Resume your hike after the vista by turning right and walking northeast along the paved McCall Dam Road. You have a choice of two trails:

1) You can turn right after 200 feet, and continue following the red blazes of Lookout Trail north and east. This coincides with part of the 9-mile ski loop and may have other markers on it in winter. The trail is easy to follow through the shady woods, but quite rocky in sections. You reach the powerline in 15 minutes. Follow it left through blueberries, ferns, mountain laurel. Turn right, off the powerline, at a double red blaze on a post. Then look for the yellow-blazed Boiling Springs Trail and a gate on the right.

2) The other choice, after the vista, would be to stay on McCall Dam Road for about 1/4 mile (5 minutes), until you reach the signed and gated Boiling Springs Trail, and follow yellow blazes the rest of the way. This trail coincides with a snowmobile trail, so other markers may be present. Turn right (east) on this wide grassy trail, lined with blueberry which ripens in July. You cross the powerline in about 10 minutes, depending on how long you linger over the blueberries. The trail curves southward, passes the signed, blue-blazed, "Old Tram Trail", and reaches the gate.

Either choice of trails is about the same distance. The red trail has more shade and less road walking, but is rockier. The yellow trail is more exposed to the sun but has a lot of blueberries, and is much easier walking.

Whichever path you came by, you are now at the gate on Boiling Springs Trail, about 1 mile (1/2 hour) from your hike's end. Go around the gate and descend on the yellow-blazed trail to Boiling Springs. A spring house covers this water supply for the park. Despite the name, and the bubbles, the water is delightfully cool.

Continue down a little way on a service road. Look sharp to find where the trail turns right. Continue following the yellow blazes southwest on an old tramway. Cross Sand Mountain Road diagonally and continue in the same direction, across another paved park road and go to the main activities area of the park: near the beach, concessions, picnic shelters, restrooms and playground. The new Environmental Center building is about 500 feet uphill from here, near the northside parking area. To return to your car, go down past the beach and turn left across the footbridge where you started.

CHAPTER 41
QUEHANNA WILD AREA
High and Mighty Pretty

Summary: 5 miles/ 3 hours walking; or any length you choose. Moderately easy walking on the high Allegheny Plateau. Hike or x-c ski in Pennsylvania's largest Wild Area.

Location: 37 miles NW of State College. Start from PA 26 N.

Features: On this high plateau above 2000 feet, snow can be found early and late in winter. A northern forest type of beech, cherry, maple, and birch covers much of Quehanna, distinct from the oak and laurel vegetation found in the Ridge and Valley region of Pennsylvania. Remote from the cities, it teems with wildlife. Quehanna is a very big place. The State Forest Wild Area within the 16-sided polygon contains 48,186 acres. Two State Natural Areas, Marion Brooks and Wykoff Run, as well as parts of State Gamelands #34 are located within or nearby. The Quehanna hiking trail forms a 75-mile loop from Parker Dam State Park on the west to Sinnemahoning on the east. Two north-south Cross Connector Trails and many miles of x-c ski trails provide smaller loops.

History: The Quehanna Wild Area was originally established as an industrial area in the mid-1950s. Curtiss-Wright Corporation used this isolated location to test jet engines and experiment with a nuclear-powered airplane. All existing hunting camps were removed then. Later the area was designated a State Forest Wild Area, set aside for the general public to enjoy "hiking, hunting, fishing and the pursuit of peace and solitude".

The Quehanna Trail and its Cross Connectors were made in 1975-76 with Federal Title 10 Funds through the YCC program. Some work was done later by the Quehanna Trail Club from Clearfield, and by State Forest personnel.

On May 31, 1985 a tornado cut a devastating mile-wide swath across the entire 50-mile length of the area. The newly established KTA TrailCare Team came to the rescue and reopened the QT near Parker Dam. During the 1990's KTA provided volunteer labor to build bridges on Mix Run, Gifford Run and Medix Run. Penn State Outing Club's X-C Ski /Division has also worked steadily to establish the network of blue-blazed ski trails.

A comprehensive guide to Quehanna, called *"Greate Buffaloe Swamp"*, by Ralph Seeley, was published in 1995 by Quehanna Area Trails Club. This book not only describes the trails, but offers considerable historical background of the area. Combined with the DCNR Bureau of Forestry map of Quehanna Trail, it is an interesting and very useful resource for Quehanna hikers.

To become an overseer, or to obtain more information about Quehanna Wild Area trails, call or write Ralph Seeley, 2025 Halfmoon Valley Rd., Port Matilda, PA 16870, phone: (814)692-8223 or Quehanna Area Trails Club, c/o Edith Hebel, HC1 Karthaus 16845, phone: (814)263-4286.

Other maps: USGS topo, Devils Elbow, Driftwood, The Knobs, & Benezette quads; Moshannon S.F. map; Elk S.F. map; Quehanna Trail map by DCNR Bureau of Forestry; PSOC map #158. See also, *Greate Buffaloe Swamp* by Ralph Seeley; *50 Hikes in Central PA* by Tom Thwaites, and *Pennsylvania Hiking Trails* by KTA.

Getting there: Quehanna W.A. is 25 miles north of Black Moshannon, a 50-mile drive from State College. Take PA 26 and PA 150 north to Milesburg. Either use I-80 or follow PA 144 NW to Snow Shoe and Moshannon. Follow PA 879 through Karthaus; turn right on Quehanna Highway, through Piper, into Wild Area. The tornado swath may still be discernible as an area of thinner forest, which changes abruptly at the Clearfield/ Cameron County line. Soon you reach Wykoff Run Natural Area at Wykoff Run Road on the right. Parking is on the left (SW) of the highway.

Hike description #1: A 5-mile Bellefonte Posse/ David Lewis Loop begins here. Head south and find the blue blazes and signs which will lead you clockwise south and west through varied savannahs, woods, boulder fields, and back north along Panther Run, where you might find beaver, wood ducks, and sundews. The return leg eastward is on the David Lewis Trail, an old road.

Hike description #2: Another short hike, 4 miles out and back, from this parking spot would take you through the Wykoff Run Natural Area, located on the northeast side of the highway. Just follow the blue blazes along Old Hoover Road, graced with the white birch trees. You pass a concrete bunker which was the site of jet engine testing in the 1950s. When you reach the newer dirt road, turn around and return.

Hike description #3: For further adventures in Quehanna, drive one more mile along Quehanna Highway. Turn left on Reactor Road at a sign for Perma Grain Products. This industry which manufactures hardwood flooring is the only one still operating in Quehanna. In about 0.7 mile find a trailhead parking on the left, with a sign for the David Lewis Trail. Across Reactor Road a blue-blazed trail heads off through huckleberry northwest into the woods. From this spot connections can be made with Meeker, PSOC, Red Run, Mosquito Creek, the eastern Cross Connector, and many other trails. It is 5 miles one way to the great Mosquito Creek Bridge (1987). Carry a map with you and leave a plan with someone before you start.

Hike description #4: The next major parking is at Marion Brooks Natural Area. Back on the Quehanna Highway, continue northwest another 4 miles (5 miles past Wykoff Run), and park at the monument near the white birch grove. An interesting 3.5-mile loop begins here. Cross the highway and head south following the blazes on the MB Link and the Cross Connector. In about a mile you will pass near the Beaver Run Shallow Water Impoundment.

This black water pond creates habitat for fish and wildlife in abundance. Tree swallows swoop across the water, and a great blue heron haunts the shallows. Deer come to drink at dawn. Please, tread lightly through this special place, and keep it habitable for the wildlife and enjoyable for people. Turn left at the dam and leave the blazed trail. Walk across the dam and follow the road out past a parking area to the highway. Turn left and walk along facing traffic about 1000 feet to the sign for the Cross Connector at Paige Run. Turn right and follow blue blazes down across a bridge and up through scattered boulders. Turn left on Losey Link, and left again when you reach Losey Road. Follow the dirt road less than 1/2 mile back to your car at Marion Brooks.

Hike description #5:   A 5-mile shuttle hike can be arranged on Mix Run Trail, which follows the very beautiful trout stream and had three new bridges in 1992. Start on Mosquito Creek Trail near Deible Road, 1.5 miles west of Marion Brooks. Head north on the blue blazes until you reach the main Quehanna Trail, blazed orange. Follow it west passing Rattlesnake Vista (caution), and down Deible Run to Mix Run. The trail then turns upstream about 3.5 miles until you find a dirt road (Grant Rd.) which is just off the Quehanna Highway. Your shuttle car should be there, or at nearby Jack Dent Road or Ardell Road.

This is just a sample. Quehanna holds enough hiking to keep a short hiker, or a long one, happy for a long time.

* * * * * * * * * *

Now that you have hiked all the easier trails, it is time to branch out, to go farther afield, to stretch your capabilities. *The Short Hiker* provides just enough information to get you started. The rest is up to you.

MAP FOR QUEHANNA - west

MAP FOR QUEHANNA -east

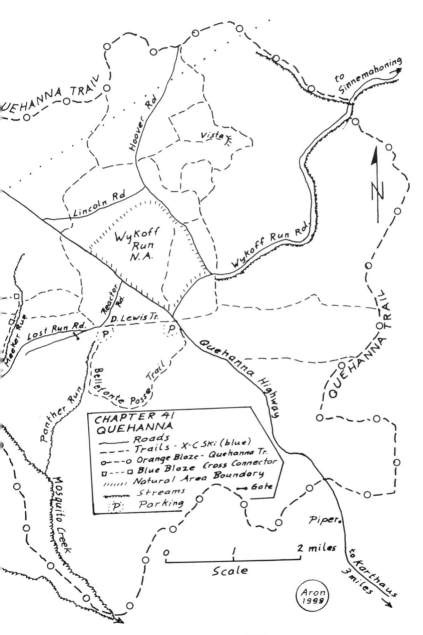

CHAPTER 41
QUEHANNA
——— Roads
– – – Trails - X-C Ski (blue)
o—-o Orange Blaze - Quehanna Tr.
□---□ Blue Blaze Cross Connector
///// Natural Area Boundary
~~~~ Streams
☐ Gate
P: Parking

2 miles
Scale

Aron
1999

THE WEB OF NATURE
(c) 1980 Jean Aron

A delicate treasure of sudden delight
hung shimmering silver in morning light.

An exploring ray of sunlight angled its way through
hemlock boughs entangled, and caught the dewdrop
prisms clinging to tiny rows of silken stringing,
reflecting back to our grateful eyes a kaleidoscope of a
million skies -- a visual explosion of icy mirrors
...Symmetric silence deafened our ears.

What intricate purpose, which force sublime
had struggled up through the eons of time,
and through generations of spidery creatures,
to culminate now with these marvelous features?
What brought all together, by chance or by scheme,
our eyes, and the web, and the errant sunbeam?
All our lives we had slept, but awoke with a start for this
glimpse of eternity, transcending art.

The natural world, like that silvery vision,
is balanced the same, with much care and precision.
Each strand of life depends on the all.
Break part of the web, and the whole web will fall.
No part can be taken. No part stands alone.
Each one has its purpose, each tree, leaf, and stone.
Who knows what worlds we destroy in a day
in the forests of Earth on our blundering way?

Will the web still be there for our children to see?
Or is it a memory, dying with me?

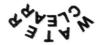

WATER CLEAR
(c) 1998 Jean Aron

We walk in quiet closeness
after the storm,
through crystal mist,
in jeweled twigs of time.

No distant views today,
no broad horizons;
but microcosmic worlds
seen upside down
in drops of rain.

Thoughts turn inward,
droplets pend expectant.

A foggy day brings home a glimpse of clarity:

Our lives, our worlds, our woes
are mostly water --

The rest is just reflection.

artwork by Steve Aron, 1987

A Short Hiker's List
of CROSS-COUNTRY SKIABLE TRAILS

REMEMBER: Valley roads may be bare, while good skiing (and bad driving) conditions persist in the mountains. Distances are approximate. You may have to ski or walk several more miles to get to certain trails, depending on snow.

Chapter 2, WALNUT SPRINGS PARK - In town accessibility makes this a good place to start, but only after fresh snow, before trampling.

Chapter 5, BOALSBURG NATURE TRAIL - Learning to ski? Museum grounds have plenty of open flat space and small hills for lessons and practice.

Chapter 7, SAND SPRING - Ski on Shingletown Gap jeep trails between Laurel Run Road and Sand Spring Trail. May require skiing 2 to 3 miles on the road first to get there from Tussey Mountain Ski Area.

Chapter 8, SKYLINE TRAIL - 3+ miles. Needs lots of snow and people to break trail. May require skiing 3.5 miles up Laurel Run Road first, and back again. Or ski down Little Shingletown Road Trail (shuttle).

Chapter 9, BIG HOLLOW - 2 to 4 miles. Ski on the rail trail or down the valley. Go early before snow is trampled.

Chapter 10, BARRENS AND GREENBRIAR - 2 to 10+ miles. Ski almost anywhere on Gamelands #176 trails. The Barrens area holds snow well. Favorite staging areas are at Scotia Target Range, or any parking area along Range Road. The 4-mile Greenbriar Loop is popular and accessible, leaving from the paved, plowed Sleepy Hollow Drive just 1 mile west of State College.

Chapter 11, TOW HILL - Ski wide gently rolling road trails, such as Tow Hill Road Trail in Gamelands. Take compass and maps.

Chapter 12, TUSSEY RIDGE - Flat; needs deep snow beyond powerline.

Chapter 13, JACKSON TRAIL - Similar to Tussey Ridge above.

Chapter 14, SOUTH IRONSTONE - 2 to 4 miles. Ski from Monroe Furnace, either direction.

Chapter 15, STONE VALLEY LAKE - 3 to 7+ miles. X-C Ski center offers lessons, rentals; new map, good trail network; good skiing, but may be over-used on weekends.

Chapter 17, WHIPPLE DAM - Ski around the lake on roads and trails

Chapter 18/19, LITTLE FLAT/ BIG FLAT - Ski on 3.5 miles of Mid State Trail on the ridge; part of a 12+ mile "bootbuster" favored by the Penn State Outing Club. Needs deep snow and several skiers to break trail. First ski several miles to get there via Lonberger Path (3 miles) and North Meadows Road (2.5 miles), plus another 3.5 miles down the roads from Little Flat Tower.

Chapter 20, BEAR MEADOWS - 3.5 miles. Circumnavigate the bog on "Meadows Trail". Fairly flat; but wet. First ski 3.5 to 4 miles to get there, if Bear Meadows Road is not driveable.

Chapter 21, JOHN WERT PATH - 3 to 7 miles. Beautiful, flat but curvy. A walk on skis. First ski 4 miles on Lonberger, or Bear Meadows Rd.

Chapter 22, DETWEILER RUN ROAD - 2 to 7 miles. Ski on the gated old road; 2 miles to the pipeline, 4 miles to the head of Detweiler Valley, or continue down Thickhead Mountain Rd. to Penn Roosevelt. Easy skiing, but difficult to reach in winter.

Chapter 23, ALAN SEEGER - 3 to 4 miles. Ski the jeep trails off Seeger Road south of the park. Drive to Alan Seeger via McAlevy's Fort.

Chapter 25, COLYER LAKE - Ski around the lake, or on it when frozen.

Chapter 26, CENTRE HALL MOUNTAIN. If you can get there, you may be able to ski some of the flatter trails. Experiment.

Chapter 27, BLACK MOSHANNON PARK - 5 to 10 miles.
  Ski Moss Hanne Trail, the pipeline off PA 504, and other park trails. High plateau holds snow well; gets heavy use.

Chapter 28, ALLEGHENY FRONT TRAIL - The part from Julian Pike to Underwood Road may be skiable.

Chapter 29, ROCK RUN TRAIL - 6 to 12 miles. Located 5 miles northeast of Black Moshannon Park. Built as a cross-country ski trail. Very wild, but improving. Remote area. Skiers should be well prepared. This trail is not for the novice.

Chapter 30, GREENWOOD FURNACE - 2 to 5 miles. New Brush Ridge X-C Ski Trails, from Forestry parking lot off Broad Mtn. Rd., offer the easy 2.2-mile Black Lick Run Loop, or the advanced 5-mile Brush Ridge Trail Loop. Tramway Trail is skiable, but does not hold snow well.

Chapter 34, BALD EAGLE PARK - 3 to 5 miles. Ski the Lakeside Trail. or the Butterfly Trail, or the 4-mile hike/x-c ski trails north of PA 150.

Chapter 37, LOWER TRAIL - 1 to 11 miles. Good beginner trail; scenic but flat; no hills, you will have to ski all the way. Accessible on paved plowed roads.

Chapter 38, CANOE CREEK - Open spaces for beginners. Moores Hill Trail is too steep, but check the other park trails. Lower Trail plans to extend into Canoe Creek in the near future.

Chapter 39, PRINCE GALLITZIN. - Most of the park trails would be skiable; may need 8+ inches of snow. Drive via Altoona.

Chapter 40, R.B. WINTER PARK - 9 miles. Ski Halfway Loop, or PSOC trails on Shriner Mountain.

Chapter 41, QUEHANNA WILD AREA - 5 to 10 miles or more. Drive 50 miles north from State College. High plateau holds snow well. Many new trails opened by PSOC X-C Ski Division. Get map from PSOC, or Bureau of Forestry, Moshannon District.

OTHER SOURCES OF MAPS AND INFORMATION

Books: (Alphabetical by author.)

- *Outbound Journeys in Pennsylvania* by Marcia Bonta, 1987
- *More Outbound Journeys in Pennsylvania* by Marcia Bonta, 1995
- *Pennsylvania Hiking Trails* by KTA 12th edition, 1998
- *Viewer's Guide to Pennsylvania Wildlife* by Kathy & Hal Korber
- *Newcomb's Wildflower Guide* by Lawrence Newcomb
- *Field Guide to Wildflowers* by Roger Tory Peterson
- *Pennsylvania's Great Rail-Trails* by Rails-toTrails Conservancy, 1994
- *Birds of North America* by Robbins, Bruun, Zim, Singer
- *Greate Buffaloe Swamp* by Ralph Seeley, 1995
- *Fifty Hikes in Central Pennsylvania* by Tom Thwaites, 3rd ed. 1995

Clubs:

- CLEARWATER CONSERVANCY, P.O. Box 163, State College, PA 16804. phone: 814-237-0400. *www.clearwaterconservancy.org*
- KEYSTONE TRAILS ASSOCIATION - (KTA), P.O. Box 251, Cogan Station, PA 17728. *www.reston.com/kta/kta.html*
- MID STATE TRAIL ASSOCIATION - (MSTA) P.O. Box 167, Boalsburg, PA 16827.
- MOUNT NITTANY CONSERVANCY, P.O. Box 296, State College, PA 16804
- PENN STATE OUTING CLUB - (PSOC) Room 8, IntraMural Building, University Park, PA 16802. Phone 814-865-2472 *www.clubs.psu.edu/outing/*
- PENNSYLVANIA NATIVE PLANT SOCIETY (PNPS), Box 281, State College, PA 16804. Watch for future web page: c/o Centre County Historical Society. *http://centrecountyhistory.org/*
- RAILS-To-TRAILS of CENTRAL PA, Box 592, Hollidaysburg, 16648
- RIDGE AND VALLEY OUTINGS CLUB, 3098 Westover Drive, State College, PA 16801. Phone 814-867-7862 (RVOC). Check the RVOC outings web page at   *www.countrystore.org/rec_arts/*
- QUEHANNA AREA TRAILS CLUB - (QATC) HC1 Karthaus, PA 16845. Buy R. Seeley's book, *Greate Buffaloe Swamp*. $6.50 ppd
- SHAVER'S CREEK ENVIRONMENTAL CENTER, 508A Keller Bldg., University Park, PA 16802 , phone 814-863-2000 or 814-667-3424. *www.outreach.psu.edu/ShaversCreek/*
- STATE COLLEGE BIRD CLUB. *http://scbirdcl.affiliate.audubon.org/*

Commercial:

- PURPLE LIZARD PUBLISHING - P.O. Box 1082, Lemont, PA 16851. Recreational maps of State College and Penn State, 1997
- BOOK STORE at Greenwood Furnace State Park, RR2 Box 118, Huntingdon, PA 16652, phone 814-667-1805
- BOOK STORE at Shaver's Creek Environmental Center - (SCEC)
- SUPPLY STORE - Appalachian Ski and Outdoors, 324 West College Ave., State College, PA 16801. 814-234-3000.
- SUPPLY STORE - Tussey Mountain Outfitters, 226 North Water Street, Bellefonte, PA 16823. phone: 814-355-5690

Government:

- CENTRE REGION PARKS AND RECREATION DEPARTMENT, 131 South Fraser Street, State College, PA 16801. Phone 814-231-3071; Senior Citizens 814-231-3076.
- PA DEPT. of CONSERVATION & NATURAL RESOURCES, (DCNR) *www.dcnr.state.pa.us/*

DCNR Bureau of Forestry, P.O. Box 8552, Harrisburg, PA 17105.
    phone: 717-783-7941
Rothrock District #5, Box 403, Huntingdon, PA,16652, 814-643-2340.
Bald Eagle District #7, Box 147, Laurelton, PA 17835, 717-922-3344.
Moshannon District #9, Box 952, Clearfield, PA 16830, 814-765-0821.

DCNR Bureau of State Parks, PO Box 8551, Harrisburg, PA 17106.
    phone: 1-888-PA-PARKS.

- PA GAME COMMISSION, 2001 Elmerton Ave., Harrisburg, PA 17110. phone: 717-787-9612.

artwork by Steve Aron, 1987